Content Analysis

POCKET GUIDES TO
SOCIAL WORK RESEARCH METHODS

Series Editor

Tony Tripodi, DSW

Professor Emeritus, Ohio State University

JAMES W. DRISKO
TINA MASCHI

Content Analysis

Oxford University Press is a department of the University of
Oxford. It furthers the University's objective of excellence in research,
scholarship, and education by publishing worldwide.

Oxford   New York
Auckland   Cape Town   Dar es Salaam   Hong Kong   Karachi
Kuala Lumpur   Madrid   Melbourne   Mexico City   Nairobi
New Delhi   Shanghai   Taipei   Toronto

With offices in
Argentina   Austria   Brazil   Chile   Czech Republic   France   Greece
Guatemala   Hungary   Italy   Japan   Poland   Portugal   Singapore
South Korea   Switzerland   Thailand   Turkey   Ukraine   Vietnam

Oxford is a registered trademark of Oxford University Press
in the UK and certain other countries.

Published in the United States of America by
Oxford University Press
198 Madison Avenue, New York, NY 10016

Cataloging-in-Publication data is on file at the Library of Congress
ISBN 978-0-19-021549-1

1 3 5 7 9 8 6 4 2
Printed in the United States of America
on acid-free paper

Contents

Preface

We are very pleased to have *Content Analysis* join the Oxford Pocket Guides to Social Work Research Methods series. Content analysis is a widely used research method in social work and in allied disciplines and professions. As of March 2015, the *Social Work Abstracts* database showed 551 publications in which "content analysis" was used as a specific research method. Content analysis is often included in social work textbooks, such as those by Rubin and Babbie (2010), Maschi and Youdin (2011), Royce (2013), and Engel and Schutt (2013). However, the textbook discussions of content analysis fall short of clarifying some important variations within the method and in conveying its wide-ranging application to different types of data. The textbook portrait of content analysis unduly limits researchers in understanding the method, its strengths, its optimal uses, and its limitations.

This Oxford Pocket Guide offers a comprehensive overview of the variety within content analysis, along with detailed descriptions of three approaches found in the contemporary literature. This book provides an inclusive and carefully differentiated examination of contemporary content analysis purposes and methods. Such a book is not currently available in the social work literature. This book also includes many illustrations of actual content analyses, along with two full-length studies reviewed in detail. In this way, we hope the book is both conceptual and practical, guiding the planning of projects as well as the methods to realize their completion. We hope it will be useful to researchers familiar with some forms of the method and will educate those new to content analysis.

In this book, we describe and examine three key approaches to content analysis: (1) basic content analysis, which focuses on manifest content and employs statistical analyses, in contrast to (2) interpretive content analysis, which focuses on both manifest and latent content, and (3) qualitative content analysis, which also focuses on both manifest and latent content. Interpretive and qualitative content analyses draw on narrative analysis methods rather than statistical analyses. Content analytic is neither simple nor monolithic. Understanding the multiple approaches to content analysis now available provides researchers with more choices, greater utility, and enhanced rigor for their projects. Our objective in this book is to help researchers expand their knowledge and fully understand the range of available tools in order to generate better research results.

The three methodology chapters of the book (Chapters 2, 3, and 4) are organized by a consistent outline. Several issues are explored in the same order to differentiate and examine the three approaches to content analysis. For each approach, we address the research purposes, intended audiences, epistemological issues, ethical issues, research designs, sampling techniques, coding techniques, analytic techniques, and the role of researcher self-reflection and reflexivity. Coupled with multiple examples of published studies, this organization can help readers better understand how the three approaches to content analysis are alike or different.

First, we draw a distinction between more *basic* content analyses drawing on literal and manifest content and *interpretive* and *qualitative* approaches that emphasize both context and latent content. In social work textbooks, content analysis is generally portrayed as drawing on manifest content in existing documents. This choice makes the coding process appear literal, where in practice it often requires a great deal of interpretation by the researcher. Literal, even automated, approaches to coding are indeed found in content analyses. However, most social work content analyses involve some judgments by the researcher in understating, interpreting, and coding complex data. Thus, a distinction between more basic, literal, and more interpretive approaches is fundamental to understanding the variation within traditional content analysis.

Second, there are differences among these methods based on use of deductive approaches to coding and analysis versus use of inductive approaches or use of both approaches in combination. These choices influence how coding is understood and undertaken, and they shape the analytic choices used in content analyses. We will explore content analyses using deductive, inductive, and mixed approaches.

Third, we examine the relatively new set of methods known as "qualitative content analysis." Several recent social work publications have stated that they use qualitative content analysis methods that do not involve quantification or statistics at all. Qualitative content analyses have somewhat different forms in the English-language and German literatures. However, all of these methods find usefulness in content analysis methods that emphasize context and require researcher interpretation and do not involve quantification. We hope to introduce and clarify the key elements of this innovative research method.

Fourth, the development of qualitative content analysis requires that researchers pay greater attention to distinguishing content analysis from other forms of qualitative research. One could argue that *all* qualitative research addresses content, but how and why different methods are applied warrants further conceptualization and clarification. Content analysis may share features with other qualitative (and quantitative) methods, but it is not identical to them. We will explore how qualitative content analysis differs from several other qualitative research methods.

Fifth, we examine the role of epistemology in shaping content analysis. This topic is virtually unexplored in the existing content analysis literature. A key but virtually unmentioned difference between quantitative and qualitative approaches to content analysis centers on epistemology. Most basic and interpretive content analyses appear to draw on positivist or realist epistemological positions. Yet several qualitative content analyses appear to use a constructivist epistemology. We explore such epistemological differences and their effects on content analysis methods in this book.

Sixth, another limitation of the textbook approach to content analysis is a heavy emphasis on the use of existing or secondary data. Many content analyses *do* examine existing data. However, there is also a longstanding tradition of analyzing newly generated, primary data in both quantitative and qualitative content analyses. Researchers need to understand the range of uses of content analysis to fully identify its potential for generating new knowledge. Using content analysis to examine practice through the statements of clients and professionals has a long history in the social work literature. In fact, one very early application of content analysis in social work used case records to assess the effectiveness of interventions (Dollard & Mowrer, 1947). We seek to help researchers understand the range of uses of content analysis and to illustrate how it has been used in social work and allied professions.

Seventh, we will provide many exemplars of content analyses from the literature and other sources. We hope to *show* how researchers actually *do* content analysis along with *telling* a lot about *how* it is done. The concluding chapters offer detailed descriptions of two content analyses. In addition, each chapter includes summaries of several exemplar studies linked to the content being discussed. This should also make the book clear and useful for classroom teaching.

Eighth, the concluding chapters examine how content analysis can be used in advocacy efforts. Researchers often use content analyses as a data source in support of advocacy efforts. Analysis of documents and newly collected narratives both provide a valuable evidence base for claiming that greater attention is needed to a specific area of interest. Content analyses of both existing and newly collected data can be used in needs assessment, clarification of practice processes and consumer views, and even as a screening tool for some problems. In this way, content analysis fits well with social work practice needs.

Finally, we examine the strengths and limitations of two full-length exemplar studies to illustrate the variety and complexity of content analysis. Many studies are described in considerable detail throughout each chapter of this book. We hope this book will be useful as a refresher for those already familiar with content analysis and as a useful introductory text for those who are learning the methods or its variants.

James W. Drisko, PhD, LICSW
Smith College School for Social Work,
Northampton, Massachusetts

Tina Maschi, PhD, LCSW, ACSW
Fordham University Graduate School of Social Service,
New York, New York

Content Analysis

Introduction

The aim of this Pocket Guide is to distinguish and examine three approaches to content analysis. Many researchers think of "basic content analysis" as a quantitative research method, which is an accurate but limited understanding. Researchers do use word counts as a core analytic technique in basic content analysis. However, researchers also use content analysis without statistical analyses in approaches called "interpretive content analysis" and "qualitative content analysis." In these two approaches, researchers focus on narratively describing the meaning of communications, in specific contexts, rather than on using quantitative word counts. These three varying approaches to content analysis have several similarities and some striking differences. They vary in the ways researchers conceptualize content and employ methods for collecting, coding, and analyzing data.

This book seeks to provide researchers with a comprehensive overview of the variety within content analysis, along with detailed descriptions of each of the three key approaches to it. In this way, the book provides an inclusive, and carefully differentiated, examination of content analysis conceptualizations, purposes, and methods. Such a book is not currently available in the social work literature. We hope it will be useful to both guide researchers familiar with some forms of the method and educate those new to content analysis.

This chapter opens by offering an inclusive definition of content analysis. This will help clarify some key terms and concepts. Each of the three approaches to content analysis will also be introduced and defined briefly. The literature reveals long-standing differences between quantitative and qualitative approaches to content analysis that are still evident in contemporary published research. This chapter also offers an examination of the origins and evolution of content analysis, as well as the development of content analysis in the social work profession. The aim of this introduction is to provide perspective on the origins, long history, and conceptual foundations of content analysis. Finally, the chapter will offer some brief examples of different approaches to content analysis in order to ground the discussion in practical examples of published research.

WHAT IS CONTENT ANALYSIS?

Krippendorff (2013, p. 24) defines *content analysis* generally as "a research technique for making replicable and valid inferences from texts (or other meaningful matter) to the contexts of their use." These inferences may address the message itself, the sender(s) of the message, the recipients of the message, or the impact of the message (Weber, 1984). Note that both Krippendorff's and Weber's definitions of content analysis go far beyond attention to only the manifest content of a message. *Manifest content* refers to what is overtly, literally, present in a communication. Neither of these definitions of content analysis specify the use of either quantitative or qualitative analytic methods. Further, researchers most often use content analysis descriptively, but they may also use it to generate new concepts and theory and to test theory (e.g., Dollard & Mowrer, 1947; discussed later in the chapter). Researchers can use content analysis to identify and document the attitudes, views, and interests of individuals, small groups, or large and diverse cultural groups. Researchers may use content analysis in evaluation work to compare communication content against previously documented objectives (Berelson, 1952).

Basic Content Analysis

Berelson (1952, p. 18), an advocate of a more literal approach, defined *basic content analysis* as "a research technique for the objective, systematic and quantitative description of manifest content of communication." Note that Berelson's definition would disallow both interpretive and qualitative approaches to content analysis that do not exclusively focus on manifest content and do not always employ quantitative techniques. Neuendorf (2002) similarly defines basic content analysis as techniques using word counts or other quantitative analytic techniques. Neunedorf's definition would also disallow both interpretive and qualitative approaches to content analysis that do not use quantitative analytic methods. Authors of basic content analysis approaches define it as using quantitative analytic techniques that only or predominantly address literal communication content. Meaningful content is assumed to be fully contained in the texts under study. The frequency of word or passage use is treated as a technique to determine the relative importance of specific content. Description and data organization are the key research purposes of such basic content analysis.

Basic content analyses are those approaches using word counts and other quantitative analytic methods to analyze data. Basic content analysts code mainly manifest data using deductively or inductively generated code lists. Quantitative criteria are used to determine the reliability and validity of the coding processes. Basic content analysts typically sample existing texts created originally by others for purposes other than the current research. They seek to be systematic, objective, and transparent.

Interpretive Content Analysis

In contrast, Osgood (1959) defines a more interpretive approach to content analysis, calling it "a procedure by which one makes inferences about sources and receivers [of communication] from evidence in messages they exchange." Holsti (1969) similarly defines content analysis more interpretively as "any technique for making inferences by objectively and systematically identifying specific characteristics of messages." In this more interpretive or inferential view of content analysis, both manifest and latent content may be considered and analyzed

(Baxter, 1991; Krippendorff, 2013; Mayring, 2000, 2010). *Latent content* refers to meaning that is not overtly evident in a communication. Latent content is implicit or implied by a communication, often across several sentences or paragraphs. Berg (2008) defines latent content as the symbolism underlying physically present data. Berelson (1952) uses semiotic theory to distinguish "denotative" and "connotative" meanings of communications in any form. Denotative meanings, the manifest content, are "first-order signifiers" (Eco, 1976) corresponding to literal, common-sense, or obvious meanings (Ahuvia, 2001; Fiske, 1982). Ahuvia (2001, p. 142) states that "connotative meanings—drawn from the latent content—are arrived at by combining individual elements in a text to understand the meaning of the whole." Latent content allows researchers to interpret the whole, or the gestalt, of the communication. Note that many forms of everyday speech, such as irony, sarcasm, and double meanings, require active interpretation of communications rather than relying solely on the manifest content.

Context is another vital component of understanding the meaning of messages. Researchers can, however, reliably and productively code latent meanings using a shared set of interpretive guidelines and by developing a shared understanding of the communication content. How researchers analyze data varies considerably but centers on narrative summaries that reveal and summarize key issues.

While Holsti (1968, p. 601) advocates for a definition of content analysis that goes beyond the quantification of manifest content, he also notes that "the differences between the broader and more restrictive views are not so great as suggested at first glance." Similarly, George (1959b) goes so far as to argue that the "manifest" or "basic" versus "interpretive" distinction may be misleading. That is, both basic and interpretive or qualitative approaches to content analysis require carefully defined and transparently reported descriptions of how the researchers collected, coded, and analyzed the target materials. All good content analysis must be systematic, methodologically based, and transparently reported. Nor is a simple quantitative versus qualitative distinction optimal. As we shall see, many content analyses actually employ both qualitative and quantitative research techniques. That is, the coding of data often involves qualitative coding techniques while the summarizing of data often involves quantitative techniques (George, 1959b). Yet some content analyses (those called interpretive and qualitative approaches) may not involve quantification or statistics at all (Bloom, 1980). Instead, they focus on summarizing and describing meanings in an interpretive, narrative manner.

Interpretive content analyses are those approaches using researcher-generated summaries and interpretations rather than word counts or other quantitative analytic methods. Interpretive content analysts code both manifest and latent or contextual communication content, typically using inductively generated code lists. Researchers use qualitative criteria to determine the reliability and validity of the analytic processes, though these quantitative terms are still employed. Interpretive content analyses typically draw upon newly generated texts, but they may also examine existing data sets. Interpretive content analyses seek to be systematic and transparent but do not necessarily assume objectivity (Ahuvia, 2001).

Interpretive content analysis shares many features with other qualitative research methods. Issues of epistemology, however, are rarely mentioned, and the use of terms such as *validity* and *reliability* are still widely used. Research methods, including sampling plans, coding procedures, and analysis plans, vary widely but mainly yield descriptive narrative summaries. While qualitative researchers now focus on the credibility and trustworthiness of studies, the interpretive content analysis literature instead emphasizes validity and reliability, perhaps following the now dated work of Kirk and Miller (1985). Interpretive content analysis may overlap with some not very well-articulated qualitative research methods such as "thematic analysis" (Boyatzis, 2000). Ginger (2006) calls interpretive content analysis a flexible research method that may explore key story lines, subjects and objects of texts, normative positions, and the methods used to claim these positions.

While both interpretive and qualitative content analysis publications are found in the social work and other literatures, the methods appear to share many features. Both approaches are still being developed and more clearly defined.

Qualitative Content Analysis

Qualitative content analysis is a relatively recent approach, with origins in German scholarship. Mayring (2000, Section 1) defines *qualitative content analysis* as "an approach of empirical, methodological controlled analysis of texts within the context of communication, following content analytical rules and step by step models, without rash quantification." Based on the interpretation of texts, focused by the researcher's chosen questions, qualitative content analysis seeks to develop carefully specified categories that are revised and refined in an interactive, feedback-loop process to ensure credibility and usefulness (Mayring, 2000, Section 2). Public justification of the analysis replaces inter-rater reliability, requiring that authors *show* their readers how the analysis was completed, with many links back to the original texts. The analysis of texts in qualitative content analysis involves both the inductive definition of categories and the deductive application of these categories to additional data (Mayring, 2000; Schreier, 2012). Mayring also exclusively cites examples of qualitative content analyses that draw on newly collected data sets, often based on interviews.

Content Analysis Across Approaches

Despite differences in emphases and in analytic techniques, there is strong agreement that *content analysis is a structured research approach, using specified research designs and methods, to make replicable and valid inferences from texts and similar materials* (Krippendorff, 1980, 2013; Mayring, 2000; Neuendorf, 2002; Schreier, 2012). While agreeing on the purposes of content analysis, the more quantitatively oriented researchers emphasize validity, reliability, and objectivity (Berelson, 1952; Berger 1991; Neuendorf, 2002; Riffe, Lacy, & Fico, 2005), while the more qualitatively oriented researchers emphasize validity, replicability, and transparency (Altheide, 1987; Altheide & Schneider, 2013; Mayring, 2000). Despite their differences in terminology, both camps argue that readers should fully understand how the researcher collected, coded, and analyzed the data in considerable detail.

Data Types and Sources

Early definitions of content analysis emphasized the analysis of written texts only, but changes in communication media now encompass a wider range of materials. While many people think of "texts" as written objects that can be "read," others view texts more broadly as objects that can be interpreted to convey an informative message. That is, to researchers, "text" actually refers to a wide range of communication media that can be stored in many different formats. Researchers have applied content analysis to texts, audio recordings, television shows and movies, images, and telephone calls, as well as to many forms of electronic data, now including social media. Researchers may transcribe some of these other materials into written texts or transcripts, but this is always done with a loss of some information. For example, transcripts of electronically recorded interviews routinely lose the speaker's prosody (rhythm of speech), tone of voice, and inflection. This constitutes a loss of information and detail from the message's original form. However, transcripts may nonetheless capture the core overt content of the message. In such cases, researchers must make choices about the importance of how the content was structured and delivered instead of emphasizing only the core content of the message.

While all content analyses focus on content, some also address form and format (Krippendorff, 1980, 2013; Schreier, 2012). For example, linguists may be interested in how a story was structured and "told" as much as in its subject content (Ahuvia, 2001).

In another example, a content analysis of the images used in advertisements or propaganda may address particular attention to where an image is located, its size, and the context in which it is placed. Similarly, inferences made from propaganda may require extensive knowledge about the history and context surrounding the message to generate a useful interpretation (George, 1959a). Researchers who seek to make valid, replicable, and useful inferences about content may adopt very narrow, or very wide-ranging, concepts of what constitutes content in communication, based on their study goals and purposes.

CONTENT ANALYSIS DEFINED

We define *content analysis as a family of research techniques for making systematic, credible, or valid and replicable inferences from texts and other forms of communication.* We find merit and worth in the application of basic, interpretive, and the more recent qualitative approaches to content analysis. Rigorous content analysis must be based on a systematic approach that is clearly described to the reader and that allows replication by other researchers. As we shall see, which specific methods will prove most revealing and most useful will differ by the chosen research question and research purposes to which content analysis is applied.

An examination of the origins and development of content analysis methods, discussed next, offers valuable perspective on the method. Content analysis has evolved and diversified as its uses have expanded over time. Content analysis includes several methodologies addressing different research purposes.

THE ORIGINS AND HISTORY OF CONTENT ANALYSIS

The early origins of content analysis are found in political differences and in advocacy efforts. Krippendorff and Bock (2008) point to an early form of content analysis addressing differences in the content of religious hymns. In 1743, the Swedish state church was concerned that the content of hymns created by unsanctioned sources differed from their formally approved content. Dovring (1954–1955) examined several approaches to analyzing the content of the hymns used during the controversy. While contemporary analysts found few actual differences in the content of sanctioned and unsanctioned hymns, methods of counting words and the context of their usage anticipated what have become the core methods of today's content analysis. Formal and detailed in tone, church officials used these content analyses to inform their decision-making processes. They also used these analyses to inform wider public discussion and advocate in favor of their decisions. The summary description of actual hymn content was a useful, empirically based part of a larger disagreement.

Krippendorff and Bock (2008) also found an early form of content analysis in a political commentary published in the *New Hampshire Spy* newspaper, on November 30, 1787. In this commentary, the unnamed author summarizes the elements ("a recipe") of an anti-Federalist essay. The author states that such essays should include the term "well-born" nine times, "aristocracy" 18 times, "liberty of the press" 13 times, and so on. The author goes on to say that this catalog of elements may be "dished up at pleasure" (in any order) to create an anti-Federalist essay (see Figure 1.1).

Krippendorff and Bock (2008, p. 1) state that the *Spy* article is "part political commentary, part literary criticism, and part effort to justify

NEW-HAMPSHIRE SPY

Vol. III.)   F R I D A Y,   November 30, 1787.   (No. 11

*A R*eceipt *for an* Anti federal Essay

WELL-BORN, nine times—*Ariftocra-*
cy, eighteen times—*Liberty of the Prefs*
thirteen times repeated—*Liberty of Con-*
fcience, once—*Negro flavery,*once mentioned—*Trial by Jury,* feven times—*Great*
Men, fix times repeated—Mr. Wilson,
forty times—and laftly, George Mason's
*RightHand in a Cutting-Box,*nineteen times
—put them altogether, and difh them up
at pleafure. Thefe *words* will bear boil-
ing, roafting, or frying—and, what is re-
markable of them, they will bear being
ferved,after being once ufed,a dozen times
to the fame table and palate.

Figure 1.1. Word counts create a "recipe" for an anti-Federalist essay (1787).

the argument." Humorous and sarcastic in tone, the article is intended
for a mass public audience and makes a clear if somewhat indirect advocacy point. Yet, in contrast to today's methodologically rigorous content
analyses, the article lacks a clear and transparent methodology showing
the reader how, and on what evidence, the investigators constructed the
summary. Nonetheless, it communicates content, a point of view, and is
a form of advocacy.

Beyond the specific content, the visual presentation used in the *Spy*
article may be familiar to some readers. The visual presentation is similar in format to today's "word clouds," or weighted lists used in newspapers to display the frequency of specific words used in articles (Halvey &
Keane, 2007) (see Figure 1.2). *The New York Times* used an "inaugural
words" (2011) word cloud to detail the word use frequency in President
Obama's first inaugural address. The larger the font size, the more frequently the word was used within the speech. Use of highlighting indicates that the specified word was used more than the average frequency

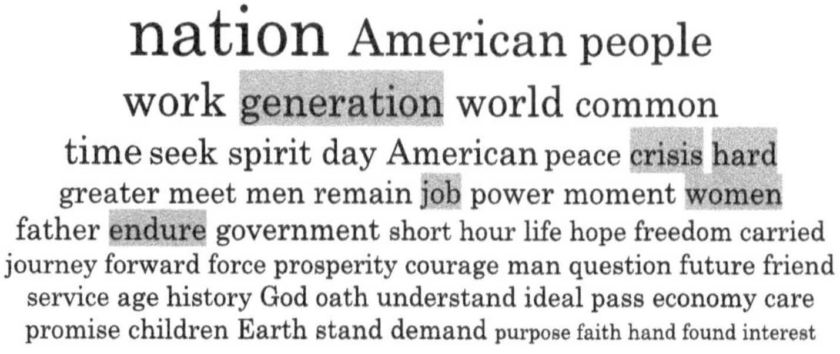

nation American people
work generation world common
time seek spirit day American peace crisis hard
greater meet men remain job power moment women
father endure government short hour life hope freedom carried
journey forward force prosperity courage man question future friend
service age history God oath understand ideal pass economy care
promise children Earth stand demand purpose faith hand found interest

From *The New York Times* (July 3, 2011).

Figure 1.2. A "word cloud" in which larger font size reflects greater word use.

across all presidential inaugural addresses ("Inaugural words," 2011). Content analysis and word clouds are useful ways to make points and to summarize large volumes of data. Word clouds share with basic content analysis the use of word counts to describe and analyze textual data.

THE ORIGINS OF ACADEMIC CONTENT ANALYSIS

The early origins of formal academic content analysis appear in the 1910s, in sociology and journalism. Krippendorff and Bock (2008) state that in a speech to the first congress of German sociologists in 1910, Max Weber advocated for the formal analysis of newspaper content. Weber sought formal research to describe and document the changes in newspaper content across generations. He specifically pointed to the merits of analyzing advertisements as a source of data to describe trends in social change. Perhaps building on Weber's suggestion, Tenney, a journalism professor, called in 1913 for comprehensive content analysis of the press to determine national and regional differences in interests and concerns. These calls for action unfortunately preceded the availability of adequate technology to undertake formal content analyses. Still, they set the stage for the development of specific content analysis methods.

By the 1940s, several disciplines and professions used content analysis. Content analyses of newspaper articles and advertisements by journalists and sociologists were growing in number and quality. Gordon Allport (1942), a psychologist, applied content analysis to case studies.

He applied content analysis to the letters of an Irish immigrant to the United States in an effort to understand her personality (Allport, 1965). This work began the application of content analysis to the study of personality and diagnosis. During World War II, content analysis was employed by Allied governments to examine military intelligence. De Sola Pool (1960) described how wartime content analysis combined the detailed description of communication content, extensive knowledge of the contemporary context, and the use of interpretive methods to extract the most useful information from enemy propaganda. Notably, the use of contextual factors to make relevant and useful interpretations from content was vital to the effectiveness of this effort. Not just the details of manifest content but also its fit within a matrix of background data was vital to making the most accurate and useful interpretations. Military intelligence work expanded content analysis from summarizing and describing overt media content to include a more interpretive, holistic, and contextual analytic approach.

Content Analysis in Social Work

Content analyses appeared in the social work literature in the 1940s. The New York Community Service Society hired psychologists Dollard and Mowrer to evaluate casework service effectiveness. Dollard and Mowrer (1947) hypothesized that casework effectiveness could be demonstrated through the reduced use of distress-related words by clients. That is, they hypothesized that clients' reduced use of distress words would demonstrate improvement compared to pretreatment status. They then developed a measure called the Discomfort-Relief Quotient, based on the frequency of word use found in client case records. This measure was simply the number of "discomfort" comments found in case records divided by the number of "discomfort plus relief" comments. Of course, to calculate this measure, each case record had to be carefully read and coded. Further, Dollard and Mowrer had to first identify a list of words that reflected various kinds of distress, along with a list of words or phrases that reflected relief. They found that their method was reliable and that several words, phrases, or complete sentences were equally reliable for calculating the measure. However, they also found that different raters could produce very different results when studying the same content. These results showed the need for thorough coder training and ongoing efforts to establish the reliability or consistency of content analysis coding. Dollard and Mowrer's work added to the development of methods and measures for more formal and rigorous content analysis.

Note that unlike many content analyses found in the literature, Dollard and Mowrer used newly generated data as the source in their content analytic work. Content analysis examines not only existing or secondary texts and materials. Dollard and Mowrer showed that in content analysis one can usefully examine newly generated data. Their work also provided an evidence-grounded method for the evaluation of social work practice.

A wide range of early work established the usefulness of content analysis and began the development of formal and rigorous research techniques. Both informal and formal content analyses are quite common in contemporary social work research and in mass media publications. Varied approaches to content analysis are now widely found in the literatures of several disciplines and professions.

Content Analysis Today

Informal content analyses are likely to be familiar to most professional and lay readers. Contemporary newspaper articles frequently summarize how the media characterizes a politician, a sports figure, or an artist over a certain period of time. For example, researchers might use an analysis of the verbs used in newspaper articles describing the President in the two previous weeks as a rough indicator of popularity. With a more narrow focus, such an analysis might summarize recent support for a specific policy initiative. Many negatively connoted verbs would indicate dislike or disapproval; many positive verbs would indicate liking or support. Of course, a mix of both would indicate split support. Such analysis of available data allows researchers to make evidence-grounded inferences about other issues as well (Riffe, Lacy, & Fico, 2005). In turn, such evidence can be used for advocacy to shape and influence policy and practice.

Formal content analyses draw on this general approach but require much greater rigor and specificity. Just what materials are included, and why, must be carefully determined. Just what materials researchers code as meaningful, and how they go about this coding, must also be justified and clearly defined. Finally, how researchers summarize the data must be rigorously determined. Research applications of content analysis should be transparent in methods, valid, and replicable.

An often-unrecognized strength of content analysis is that it may (though does not always) draw upon data that were not created specifically for research purposes. That is, the data used in most basic content analysis studies are naturalistic in origin. Researchers usually select such data sets for content analysis in part because other people created the material for purposes other than research. Some scholars argue that using data originally created for purposes other than research minimizes the possibility of researcher-generated bias in the data set. Still, researchers must take care in selecting suitable samples for content analysis as well as to code and analyze this material thoroughly and consistently. Another advantage of using many public forms of secondary data is that institutional human subjects review processes may not be required. Of course, ethical research using newly generated data for content analysis will require a formal human subjects review process in most instances.

Basic content analysis may be viewed as a hybrid research approach. It routinely involves coding unstructured data, which is a core technique of qualitative research. However, the coded data are most often analyzed and reduced using descriptive statistics, a core technique of quantitative research. Thus, content analysis requires knowledge and skills derived from both qualitative and quantitative research. It is a research method that combines *techniques* from both research traditions. In contrast, what researchers call "mixed methods" today purposefully integrates entire, distinct, quantitative, and qualitative studies (Creswell & Plano Clark, 2010). Mixed method research employs *complete quantitative and qualitative research studies* within a project to gain different perspectives on the study question. Content analysis may combine qualitative and quantitative *techniques* into a single study method (Creswell, 2011). It is more of a hybrid or blended research methodology than a true form of mixed methods research combining separate qualitative and quantitative studies.

EXAMPLES OF SOME SOCIAL WORK CONTENT ANALYSES

To orient the reader fully, it is useful to illustrate and examine briefly a few content analyses found in the social work literature. Such an examination can help identify the key features of content analysis. It also helps in exploring the strengths, and some potential limitations, of the method. Finally, this brief examination will clarify the research purposes to which researchers apply content analysis.

Horton and Hawkins (2010) completed a basic content analysis of intervention research reported in social work dissertations. The authors deductively developed a coding list of terms that they argue encompasses the concept of intervention research. They then examined the 252 social work dissertations completed in the year 2006. They found that 13.49% of these dissertations focused on social work practice interventions. Calling this a small percentage in this era of evidence-based practice, the authors argue for a change in social work education. They then advocate for much greater emphasis on education about, and dissertation research on, social work practice interventions.

The evidence on which the authors' conclusions were drawn is clear and replicable. Scholars might argue for different definitions of intervention research, but the authors describe how they operationalized and coded the term. However, it may be that 2006 was a year with relatively few, or relatively numerous, dissertations on intervention research when compared to other years. A larger sample including more years might provide similar or very different results. Further, whether 13.49% of dissertations on social work interventions is too low, about right, or too high an emphasis on intervention research may also be a matter of judgment. Yet the data provided are clear and lead to a transparent result used to support the author's interpretation. Other scholars could fully replicate Horton and Hawkins' work, though they might differ from the original authors' advocacy recommendations.

It is important to note that Horton and Hawkins' conclusion that 13.49% of dissertations addressing intervention research is too low represents an abductive inference that goes well beyond the reported data (Krippendorff, 2013). An *abductive argument* links an observation with a hypothesis that reasonably accounts for or explains the observation (Reichertz, 2010). In abductive reasoning, the premises do not guarantee the validity of the conclusion. It is an inference only to a plausible explanation. Horton and Hawkins describe social work dissertation content in 2006, but they do not empirically identify an appropriate or optimal percentage .of dissertations focused on intervention research. The authors add their own normative judgment that, given the importance of practice to social work profession, 13.49% is too low. They then use this abductively generated inference to advocate for more dissertation work focused on intervention research. Krippendorff (2013) notes that such abductive inferences are common in content analysis publications.

Content analysis projects require careful training of coders to ensure that they are coding the same content. Fairly literal concepts such as intervention research may require minimal training to code, but other projects may require considerable conceptual work as well as training. Here the distinction between basic or manifest forms of content analysis that code fairly literal content and more interpretive approaches that require more extensive researcher judgments becomes more evident.

In another study, Lalayants, Tripodi, and Jung (2009) sought to examine trends in international social work research content in American research journals. They chose as their sample three U.S. social work research journals with large circulations. Their project required a clear definition of international social work research. The authors first sought to distinguish between research and non-research publications (e.g., conceptual articles, reviews, letters, etc.). This proved fairly straightforward. The authors next noted that international research encompasses a diverse body of work. They chose to deductively employ a three-part typology of international research previously developed by Tripodi and Potocky-Tripodi (2007). This typology included supranational (conducted in one country but using concepts from more than one country), intranational (often addressing migrants), and transnational (comparisons across countries) forms of international research. Raters were trained initially to understand the coding criteria to be applied in the study. This involved learning the three-part typology of international research. Two readers next independently rated each article, with 100% agreement on distinguishing research and non-research articles and 77% agreement on national versus international articles. Note that the interpretive judgments required to apply the three-part typology proved more challenging than did distinguishing research from non-research articles. The research team used discussion among the raters to resolve these differences, leading to full agreement on distinguishing national versus international content. Through this process, the authors generated a population of 707 research articles in these three research journals over the 10-year period of interest.

Lalayants, Tripodi, and Jung then compared descriptively the percentages of national and international content published between 1995 and 1999 with that found between 2000 and 2004. Between 1995 and 1999, there were 342 total articles published in the three selected journals, of which 268 (78.4%) were research articles. Of these, only 12 addressed international research. This represents just 3.5% of the total research content of the three journals studied. In contrast, between 2000 and 2004, 365 total articles were published of which 299 (81.9%) were research articles. Of the total, 23, or 6.3%, were international research articles. This is a substantial increase in the total number and percentage of publications on international research across the two time periods sampled. Differences in international research were also found among the three journals and in the types of international research they published.

Lalayants, Tripodi, and Jung (2009) concluded that there has been an overall increase in international research published in these three social work research journals between 1995 and 2004. They are careful to note that books, monographs, and other forms of publication may also include international research, and that immigration and globalization create important opportunities for social workers to undertake international research even within a single country. Based on these data and increasing globalization, they abductively advocate for still more international social work research. Note that the content analysis simply documents the trends in international research publications; it does not indicate what proportion *should* address this topic.

While Lalayants, Tripodi, and Jung were appropriately thorough in reporting their study, critics might still raise some questions. For example, critics might challenge their choice of three major U.S. social work research journals as a limited population from which to draw overall conclusions. To be fair, the authors did clearly state that there are other journals in which similar research articles might be published. Critics might also ask if these journals sought out international research in any way during this period. For example, was international research part of their journal mission, or was it mentioned in a statement of guidelines for authors? Critics might further challenge the use of two 5-year periods as adequate to compile trends in research. Ten years might seem a suitable time frame for making such an assessment, but variation across individual years might prove to be even more meaningful than an aggregated 5-year time period. Nonetheless, this content analysis is transparent in its methodology and conservative in its conclusions. This content analysis does show an increase in international research publications and variation in their approaches to international research within these three journals. It serves as a reasonable and clear basis for advocating for more attention to international research in social work.

The content analysis completed by Horton and Hawkins (2010) may be considered a basic content analysis project based on manifest data. The study of Lalayants and colleagues (2009) required somewhat more interpretive judgments by the raters, but still addressed manifest evidence. Each study drew on existing texts already in the public domain. Neither study mentioned undertaking an institutional review board process. The researchers did not generate new data sources specifically for their studies. Each study involved coding units of meaning that were deductively generated and relevant to the author's stated research purposes. The content to be coded—international versus national content and presence or absence of intervention research—was possible to identify in detail before the analysis began. The chosen analytic methods were quantitative: The researchers used descriptive statistics to aggregate and further summarize the results. Yet some content analyses require inductive development of codes after the data are examined. Such content analyses require still more interpretive judgments by the researchers.

In a third study, Drisko (2008) completed a content analysis of qualitative research content in Master's in Social Work (MSW) foundation courses. At the time of the study, qualitative research was specifically required foundation research content in all accredited social work programs in the United States. Using a national survey, Drisko collected 47 foundation research course syllabi from accredited MSW programs in the United States. No such data set was previously available.

Coding qualitative research content, however, posed some serious challenges. Just what constituted "qualitative research content" was not always obvious. While some named qualitative research methods like grounded theory were easy to identify, other content was much less clear-cut. For example, qualitative research often uses inductive processes to create codes. Many syllabi included a section called "deduction versus induction," but with no specific linkage to qualitative research. Should a researcher code this content as qualitative in nature? Many syllabi also included a section on coding, but most often as part of *measurement*—the assignment of a number to a specific datum. Should a researcher code such content as qualitative in nature? In consultation with other researchers, and in collaboration with a second coder, the author decided not to code either form of content as qualitative since each lacked a clear connection to specific qualitative research content. The researcher fully described this decision in the published article, which reduced the overall amount of qualitative content located in the analysis. Of course, critics could argue that this was not an appropriate analytic decision.

Eight percent of the 47 MSW syllabi (17%) had no qualitative research content at all. The modal (most common) amount of content was a single course session in the foundation research course. Very few syllabi included any named qualitative research approaches, such as ethnography or grounded theory. Finally, very few assignments or projects included any qualitative research content.

Drisko asserts that such minimal content on qualitative research does not allow students to learn much about qualitative research. In addition, several programs did not appear to comply with accreditation standards. Critics could argue that qualitative research should not be a priority in MSW research courses, but the content analysis does show that this content is actually very limited in foundation research syllabi used by MSW programs. It is hard to imagine that a single class session would be viewed as adequate coverage for other content required for accreditation purposes. Note that, once again, the content analysis data do not address how much course content *should* address qualitative research. Still, this content analysis is transparently presented and, given access to the syllabi used for the study, could be fully replicated by other researchers. Issues in interpretation and coding were described in detail to show readers how the key analytic decisions were made. While the researchers made interpretive judgments about coding content, the final analysis was quantitative and descriptive. Here we see that the distinction between basic and interpretive content analysis is not so clear-cut. Many content analyses draw on techniques employed in both qualitative and quantitative research.

Other social work content analyses also address issues of interpretation in coding and in data analysis. For example, Finn and Dillon (2007) report their use of content analysis in teaching social work research courses. They asked their students to examine personal ads in newspapers to answer the questions, "Do men and women portray themselves differently in singles ads?" and "Do men and women look for different things in a potential partner?" Note that both questions allow for multiple interpretations. Finn and Dillon stated that an archive of academic studies about personal ads was available to help complete this project. The archive also allowed comparison of current student findings with prior published studies. Students used a single issue of a Sunday newspaper including 169 personal ads as their project data set. Finn and Dillon directed their students to examine both the manifest content found explicitly in the ads and to make interpretations about latent content implied in the ads. Personal ads are, of course, very short and often use abbreviations. The students developed their own codes for the ads in workgroup teams. Teams compared their codes and assessed their inter-rater reliability. They then compared and contrasted their coding schemes to those found in a prior study by Willis and Carlson (1993) on sex roles in singles ads.

One can imagine that students might interpret abbreviations and short phrases in singles ads differently based on their own backgrounds, experiences, and values. They might also interpret the intended goals of the advertisers quite differently. Finn and Dillon (2007) invited their students to explore how such interpretive judgments could influence how researchers view data and the coding process. They also asked their students to compare formally their work with that of other students and with published studies. Researchers sometime call the results of such an interpretive content analysis "softer" than those of basic content analyses drawing on manifest content. Yet researchers are frequently required to make interpretive judgments about the meaning of human communications during the coding process in content analysis. Making such interpretive judgments may be quite challenging and requires careful attention. Key choice points, and the logic supporting each analytic decision, should be detailed fully in content analysis reports.

Yet basic (more literal) and interpretative content analyses share many features and techniques. They may be based on different epistemological foundations and may address different kinds of research questions. What constitutes clear and fully manifest evidence, versus evidence that is more latent and requires more attention to context and more inference, is a key question for today's content analysts. We will explore how literal and interpretative content analyses are similar and different in later chapters. We will also explore contemporary developments in qualitative content analysis in another chapter.

Having looked briefly at a few studies to introduce both basic and interpretative approaches to content analysis, we will use the next three chapters to explore each approach in greater depth. Both quantitative and qualitative researchers claim content analysis, with good reason. Its optimal use requires the researcher to make a number of informed decisions and to apply research methods rigorously. Chapter 2 will explore basic content analysis and will include an examination of the use of statistical methods in content analysis.

2

Basic Content Analysis

This chapter will examine basic content analysis. Following a brief introduction to basic content analysis, an exemplar study will be analyzed in detail. This chapter on basic content analysis and the next two chapters will explore approaches to content analysis using the same outline. This structure will guide the reader in both planning a new study and reviewing completed studies. The components of basic content analysis include (1) the research purposes of content analysis, (2) target audiences, (3) epistemological issues, (4) ethical issues, (5) research designs, (6) sampling issues and methods, (7) collecting and "unitizing" data, (8) coding methods, (9) data analysis, and (10) the role of researcher reflection. This structure will also allow comparison across the three methods of content analysis detailed in successive chapters. In combination, these 10 components can help researchers appraise the overall integrity and rigor of a content analysis proposal or of a completed project.

Basic content analysis (Weber, 1990) is the most common form found in the social work literature. It is also very common in the multidisciplinary literature. Basic content analysis is largely deductive in form. The researcher's area of interest and preliminary codes are typically developed prior to data collection and analysis drawing on existing theoretical and empirical work. Coded content tends to be largely manifest in nature. As Baxter (1991, p. 239) states, basic content analysis focuses on "content features that could be categorized with little or no interpretation by the coder." This approach also allows data collection and data reduction using computer software algorithms. Data analysis in basic content analysis is generally quantitative and centers on the use of descriptive statistics. As Weber (1990, p. 12) states, "a central idea in content analysis is that the many words of the text are classified into much fewer categories." Researchers most often use basic content analyses to examine existing texts. The results of basic content analysis are often, but not always, used to empirically document a perceived social problem and as evidence from which to abductively advocate for change.

AN EXAMPLE OF BASIC CONTENT ANALYSIS

David Wyatt, a Canadian systems analyst, sought to identify the lesbian, gay, bisexual, or transgender (LGBT) characters on English-language network and syndicated television shows (Wyatt, 2012). In a personal communication (2006), Wyatt stated that he did not undertake this work as academic research. Instead, he stated, "I was trying to do for television something similar to what the late Vito Russo did for motion pictures in his book *The Celluloid Closet*. There was no particular purpose except providing interesting information." Wyatt's research purpose was to compile data on the presence and frequency of LGBT characters on television over time. (The full listing is available online at http://home.cc.umanitoba.ca/~wyatt/tv-characters.html). Social workers might point out that Wyatt's work could be used to describe social change and to advocate for changes in the media representation of LGBT characters in mass media. Well-documented description, however, was Wyatt's chosen research purpose. Note, too, that Wyatt's cumulative work clearly details trends over time.

Wyatt (2012) chose to limit his data collection to network and syndicated television shows. Such shows, of course, have the widest potential number of viewers or markets. However, this choice may exclude locally made or independent productions with LGBT characters. The time span under study was from 1961 to the present. His list of networks included those from the United Kingdom, Australia, Canada, Ireland, New Zealand,

South Africa, and the United States, totaling 43 networks in all. This list of mainly English-speaking countries represents a sampling decision that targets countries that have a similar cultural tradition. The sample excludes many countries and cultures as well. Other countries might be more or less open to depiction of LGBT characters.

In the online report, Wyatt notes that several early television shows "dealt" with sexual orientation in single episodes, but less often were LGBT characters included on a regular basis. A change in the frequency of such characters is one form of evidence for cultural change reflecting greater comfort with and acceptance of varied sexual orientations and gender identities. Note that examining *how* the shows presented, valued, and elaborated each character was not the purpose of Wyatt's research.

Within the network and syndicated television shows, Wyatt (2012) apparently elected to examine almost all potential programs—an enormous volume of data. However, he does not offer a listing of all the shows he examined. Instead, he offers a complete list of the shows with recurring LGBT characters. This reporting choice is fully consistent with his research purpose (a descriptive listing of characters) but leaves some slight ambiguity about exactly which shows were reviewed to create the listing. He also details shows in which characters were present in only one or two episodes (not the requisite three) or in which the character's sexual orientation was not sufficiently clear to warrant inclusion. In effect, Wyatt elected to review the entire population of network and syndicated television shows aired after 1961. This sampling plan was determined and fixed at the start of his project. The sampling plan was expanded somewhat to accommodate the emergence of subscription cable television shows and networks that were not initially included in the study. It was not changed, however, in the last decade to include online videos, which were not his intended area of study. Still, new television shows within the original population of networks and syndicates were included each year as they were aired.

Wyatt found only 1 recurring LGBT character in the decade from 1961 to 1970, 58 from 1971 to 1980, 89 from 1981 to 1990, 317 from 1991 to 2000, and nearly 900 from 2001 on. This information documents numbers in each decade and establishes an increasing trend over these four decades. Wyatt's listing of television shows and characters also provides an index for other researchers who seek to locate all LGBT characters or any specific LGBT character.

In terms of coding, Wyatt does not precisely define how he determined if a character was gay, lesbian, bisexual, or transgender. Of course, many such characters are clearly and explicitly identified in the content of the show or in their own statements during the show. However, some characters, such as Jack Ritter's character on "Three's Company," are confusing. This character was allowed by the property owner to live with two women only if he was gay. However, the character was apparently not gay in his personal identity; he only played gay to trick the property owner. Certainly, the content raises the issue of gay identity and some of its possible social consequences, but the character does not identify as gay. Content analysts are often faced with such difficult coding choices. Wyatt chose to exclude this character.

There is a clear and reasonable explanation for his coding choices, including a listing of characters and shows that were "also rans" (Wyatt, 2012, section 3.0). Also ran shows had LGBT characters but did not fully meet Watt's coding criteria. For example, a character was on for only one or two episodes rather than the required three; also ran characters might show considerable ambiguity, as in gender-changing science fiction characters. On the other hand, another researcher might see a character as mocking gays, or for other reasons decide not to include this character in their list. Researchers doing content analysis often face such difficult coding decisions even within their predetermined categories.

Finally, Wyatt used a simple frequency count as the basis for his analysis. A count of very few shows with LGBT characters empirically indicates limited public representation and presence. Higher counts indicate greater presence. This is another clear and easy-to-understand basis for interpreting public presence. Still, others might see this coding choice as lacking wider context and nuance. Another researcher might count only positive characters that were not mocked or treated unsympathetically in a show.

This is the key difference between basic and both interpretive and qualitative content analysis. Basic content analysis relies mainly on frequency counts of low-inference events that are manifest or literal and that do not require the researcher to make extensive interpretive judgments. Interpretive and qualitative content analyses require greater researcher judgments in coding and in data analysis.

Along with Wyatt's fine work discussed here to introduce key issues in basic content analysis, there are very similar academic articles on the same topic. Fisher, Hill, Grube, and Gruber (2007, p. 167) summarized 2 years of behavior and talk about "non-heterosexual behaviors" on television shows. Identifying behaviors that are unambiguously LGBT "behaviors" from heterosexual "behaviors" is no simple matter. Their analysis used Bandura's (2001) social cognitive theory, which argues that exposure to vicarious experiences is one way people develop new social norms and expectations. Fisher and colleagues used an existing coding scheme developed by Kunkel et al. (1999) for the Kaiser Family Foundation. Through an inferential statistical analysis, the researchers found a slight but significant increase in nonheterosexual behavior and talk between the 2001–2002 and 2002–2003 television seasons. Adding to Wyatt's work, they found the most varied content in variety shows and in features films, and the least in cartoons and in nonfiction documentary films. Fisher et al. (2007) also discovered that more content was aired on noncommercial (i.e., paid cable) networks than on free commercial networks. They concluded that frequent comedic depictions of nonheterosexual characters may reinforce negative and devaluing stereotypes. Further, such depictions serve as a negative influence on the socialization of LGBT youth.

Fisher et al.'s and Wyatt's work are just two examples showing that content analyses come in many forms, are published in many media, and have several different research purposes.

Next we will examine the research purposes to which basic content analysis is applied. Understanding the purposes for using content analysis will enhance our understanding of the optimal uses of this method.

RESEARCH PURPOSES OF BASIC CONTENT ANALYSIS

Basic content analysis is best known as a methodology for empirically identifying and describing themes or other aspects of communication content, as well as the devices used to deliver this content (Weber, 1990). That is, content analysis may address language, content meaning, techniques of communication, specific events, or all of these simultaneously. Content analysis allows researchers to examine large amounts of data in a systematic fashion, which helps to identify and clarify topics of interest (Weber, 1990). Researchers can also use basic content analysis to determine if content is *not* present in situations where one might expect it to be. It is widely used to detail the proportion or percentage of a text or set of materials that is devoted to specific topics. This allows researchers to make evaluative comparisons of materials with established standards or goals and to establish the relative emphasis within the materials. Trends in manifest content over time may also be displayed visually and may be analyzed using statistical techniques. These are essentially *descriptive* research uses of content analysis.

Krippendorff (2013) states that authors of content analyses often use study findings as an evidence base for making abductive arguments. An *abductive argument* links an observation with a hypothesis that accounts for or explains the observation (Reichertz, 2010). In abductive reasoning the premises do not guarantee the validity of the conclusion. It is an inference only to a plausible explanation. For example, a finding that a small percentage of textbook content addresses a given topic does not automatically mean that this percentage is too small or too large. Such advocacy arguments are possible explanations or interpretations of the empirical result, but are not inherently derived from the empirical results. Basic content analyses are generally descriptive in purpose. Advocacy claims may be linked to additional, often untested, normative or explanatory concepts. Researchers and readers of content analyses must be careful to distinguish empirical results from their abductive logical extension to likely, but unconfirmed, explanations.

Researchers have also used basic content analysis comparatively, in order to distinguish groups of people by their verbal behavior. For example, Gottschalk (1995) used a basic content analysis of word frequencies in personal narratives to distinguish persons who might warrant a psychiatric diagnosis from persons who did not. Similarly, Oxman, Rosenberg, Schnurr, and Tucker (1988) used a basic content analysis to distinguish people fitting four different psychiatric diagnostic categories by the words they used most frequently. Oxman and colleagues' analysis found that their computer program could correctly distinguish people in the four different diagnostic groups based only on word-use frequencies. This work suggests that screening devices might be possible based solely on word usage, using computer software analyses of spoken or written passages.

While these works by Gottschalk (1995) and Oxman et al. (1988) were descriptive in design, they could also be used comparatively to test theories about how psychiatric diagnosis is done and what factors are most important to doing it correctly and efficiently. On this topic, an effort was made to show that the differentiated groups correlated strongly with expert diagnoses. One might infer that the content of personal narratives successfully distinguished between the specified diagnostic categories. Here content analysis was used comparatively to identify and distinguish groups of people with different characteristics.

Recent studies have used facial recognition software to distinguish real from faked expressions of pain in video vignettes. Bartlett, Littlewort, Frank, and Lee (2014) found that humans could distinguish faked pain only 55% of the time, while facial recognition software was correct 85% of the time. Bartlett and colleagues developed a coding model that used both specific features of facial expressions and the dynamics of presentation of the facial expression to improve the accuracy of correct determinations. In this instance, a content analysis of specific features of facial expressions was combined with a formal analysis of the unfolding of the expression over a few seconds to improve identification of expressions of real pain. Both content and the short-term process of its delivery were examined. The researchers developed a codebook of both facial expressions and the patterns of the form of these expressions to generate deductively the computer algorithm. While facial recognition systems have not yet proven so successful in other areas, this application of content analysis shows how it may be used as a screening tool to distinguish groups with different attributes. In this work, too, content analysis was used to compare and contrast groups, not solely to identify and describe their features. Such research may be used to test theory as well as to describe group differences.

TARGET AUDIENCES FOR BASIC CONTENT ANALYSIS

Basic content analyses are found in many disciplines and professions. They are widely used in medicine, marketing, journalism, linguistics, communications, computer science, studies of literature, ethical studies, and religious studies. Basic content analyses are well represented in education and in both health and mental health research. As such, content analyses may be used to inform and to persuade audiences about a social issue, a product, a service, or a policy position. Audiences for basic content analyses vary from advocacy groups, to marketers, to program and policy planners, business people, policymakers, and legislators.

Audiences for basic content analyses may also be other professionals or academics, since many content analyses are published in academic journals. For example, content analyses of course syllabi and textbooks are useful tools to document what is taught, and what is omitted, in specific educational programs. As such, basic content analysis can be useful in product and service development and planning, as well as in evaluating the implementation of practices, policies, and regulations. It can also be used to describe the presence, absence, or prevalence of topics in any form of communication material. Basic content analyses may also have much wider audiences such as advocacy groups and the general public. In such cases, basic content analyses are used to raise awareness and consciousness as well as to inform and educate.

EPISTEMOLOGICAL FOUNDATIONS OF BASIC CONTENT ANALYSIS

There is little explicit discussion of epistemology in the content analysis literature as a whole. Basic content analysis appears to draw on standard positivist or realist epistemologies (House, 1991; Neuendorf, 2002). Basic content analysts generally view their work as scientific in nature (Neuendorf, 2002). Often-cited authors such as Berelson (1952), Holsti (1969), and Weber (1990) strongly emphasize reliability and correspondence validity in their texts. They use terms such as *objectivity*, indicating that they view data as straightforward and unproblematic, not subject to interpretation that varies with culture or context (Berelson, 1952; Drisko, 2013a). The researcher's personal and cultural histories, social context, and research purposes are not viewed as shaping the analysis of the data in important ways. Berelson (1952), Holsti (1969), and Weber (1990) also treat data as relatively stable and unchanging. This means that such researchers expect websites carefully saved for later review to yield very similar results when another researcher tallies up the same saved data. For example, a replication study done shortly after an initial study of the licensing information provided on the same online therapists' websites should generate essentially the same findings. Correspondence between materials encompassing the same meanings establishes validity (as in criterion validity); correspondence among coders establishes reliability.

Basic content analysts also imply that there is a strong and clear equivalence between the words they study and the meanings these words convey (Neuendorf, 2002). Words are a key foundation of meaningful communication. Such a position suggests that the data are presumed to be independent of the researcher and invariant over time, location, and the cultural background of the reader. Basic content analysts do not often view data as shaped in important ways by the interests and interpretations of the data analyst. Further, even if such bias was present, they assume that it will be detectable and addressed by later researchers and scholars. Most inferences are assumed to involve a fairly literal interpretation of content with the goal of fostering a high degree of agreement among (similar) people rating the same data.

Differences in epistemology help distinguish basic content analysis from more interpretive approaches. However, the readers/consumers of basic content analyses are unlikely to find any mention of epistemology in published reports. Readers are often left to identify the epistemology applied by the researchers.

ETHICAL ISSUES IN BASIC CONTENT ANALYSIS

Given prior harms to human research participants done by well-intended researchers, it is always wise and ethically sound to seek a formal institutional review before undertaking any research involving people. Ethics review regulations in the United States allow institutional review boards to determine that studies are exempt from review where risks are no greater than everyday hazards, to allow an expedited review where risks are slight, or to require a full review where risks are more serious. Researchers doing any form of content analysis should seek review of their projects by an authorized ethics review board.

Use of existing data, as is typical of many basic content analyses, may simplify the need for review by an ethics panel or institutional review board. This is because most data are artifacts already in the public domain, with identities of authors and other persons limited by applicable laws and publishing conventions. New data are not necessarily collected; rather, the focus is on analysis of existing, public texts and materials. Only in rare cases are new data generated for specific research purposes in basic content analysis. Most national and international informed consent regulations allow exemption from review for the research use of publicly available information. Still, review should be undertaken for such studies.

Ethical issues may arise, however, where the content being analyzed is confidential or not intended for public distribution. In such cases, where the privacy interests of an organization or corporation may compete with value of the public's need to know, both legal issues and informed consent issues may arise. For example, it may be very useful for the public to know about the content of leaked corporate documents that demonstrate a potential source of harm, or that demonstrate efforts to mislead others. In such cases, researchers should seek both review and approval from a human subjects review board and the legal staff of one's own institution.

Obtaining prior informed consent is required before the collection of new, primary, research data. After obtaining institutional review board approval for the study, the researchers must also obtain informed consent directly from participants. In situations such as conference transcripts or classroom dialogue, refusal by even one participant could prohibit collection of any data in the view of some ethics review boards. This method of obtaining consent might also move users who do not wish to have their participation recorded to leave the group and lose access to a valuable resource and diverse views. Another alternative is to gain institutional review board approval and then communicate with all users, sending them complete informed consent materials. Those users who agree to participate in the research would then send a return letter or email to the researchers stating their consent (Rourke, Anderson, Garrison, & Archer, 2000). Materials generated by any users who did not consent would not be included in the research. This is a more direct, but very time-consuming solution to obtaining informed consent when collecting data in public settings.

Blurring the Public–Private Boundary: Electronic Data

A new area of concern is the use of online bulletin boards, Facebook content, Instagram images, Tweets, and similar electronic content as sources of research data. The issue is that while almost anyone can register to join such groups, the members may not view themselves as research participants. Participants may view their contributions as private, while the extraordinary ability of search engines renders them potentially publicly accessible (Eysenbach & Till, 2001). Thus, the line between what is private and what is public may be blurred for some forms of electronic data.

Use of electronic postings and similar materials for research purposes, then, may violate the principle of obtaining informed consent from research participants. Obtaining prior informed consent for using personal data for research purposes is a core principle of all professional codes of ethical conduct in research. Yet one may argue that research use of existing texts and transcripts does not put people in the role of research participants since there was no intervention by the researcher (Rourke et al., 2000). However, such data may contain identifiable private information about participants, another source of ethical concern (Eysenbach & Till, 2001). Standards regarding the ethical collection of electronic data are rapidly evolving. Researchers are advised to maintain high ethical standards and to gain the informed consent of participants *before* using their data for research purposes. Consultation with and review by an institutional ethics review board is suggested when any concerns about the protection of human research participants—including personal privacy—are possible.

Issues of anonymity are also complex in the realm of electronic communication data. Emails addresses and headers, IP identifiers (numbers that serve as the electronic addresses on the Internet), and other potential identifiers are routinely included in email communications and electronic bulletin board postings. Thus, technically, very few electronic communications allow anonymous participation (leaving no trail back to the participant). Using electronic media, confidentiality may be possible, but anonymity may be much more difficult to ensure.

Institutional review and approval should be sought when research efforts intersect with these gray and rapidly evolving areas. Social work researchers should always undertake research consistent with the principles detailed in the National Association of Social Workers (NASW) *Code of Ethics* (2008).

RESEARCH DESIGNS IN BASIC CONTENT ANALYSIS

Early basic content analysis theorists emphasized its exploratory and descriptive uses (Berelson, 1952; Holsti, 1969). However, even these early theorists suggested that content analysis can also be used in explanatory research designs. Krippendorff (2013) has identified three kinds of research designs to which content analysis is applied. These are (1) exploratory/descriptive, in which knowledge of content and contexts are operationalized and better described or defined; (2) explanatory tests of hypotheses that examine the merit and utility of specified analytical constructs; and (3) explanatory tests of discriminant function that affirm or negate the explanatory power and utility of specified constructs. All three research designs can be found in published examples of basic content analysis. In the published social work literature, however, descriptive uses of content analysis predominate.

Overall, research design is not widely mentioned in the basic content analysis literature. Most published basic content analysis texts and papers immediately address the methods they employ without any formal description of research design. For clarity, it is useful to consider the kinds of research designs used in content analysis and how they fit with the researcher's questions and purposes. Researchers use several different overall research designs in content analysis studies to achieve varied purposes successfully.

Basic content analysis studies often use an *observational research design*, in the sense that the research makes no intervention to influence participant behavior (Rosenbaum, 2010). Observational, used in this sense, indicates a lack of intervention by the researcher, rather than data collection via direct observation. Observational research designs contrast with *experimental research designs*, in which researchers make an intervention and test its effects. The research purpose of observational designs is to discover, explore, and describe the behaviors, including thoughts, feelings, beliefs, and action, of the people or artifacts being studied. Further, if the source of data is existing texts, audio, video, or other existing materials, the researcher has no real opportunity to influence participant behavior (other than to selectively sample and code the data sources).

Basic content analysis studies often employ *cross-sectional research designs*, in the sense that they explore and/or describe the characteristics of a specified sample at one point in time or over a short span of time (Mann, 2003). For example, Drisko (2008) examined the amount of qualitative research content in foundation Master's in Social Work (MSW) research syllabi for just 1 year. However, some content analysis studies may employ a *longitudinal research design* that examines variation in a sample over time. For example, Wyatt's (2012) study tracks changes in LGBT characters on television programs for over 40 years to detail variation over the years. The difference between these two designs is that Wyatt's long-term, longitudinal study clearly documents change over time, while a single-year cross-sectional study (or even a few years) is insufficient to establish such changes and trends.

Basic content analysis may also be understood as *exploratory* or *descriptive*—or both simultaneously—in terms of research design (Anastas, 1999). This dimension of research design addresses the overall purpose of the study. *Exploratory research designs* often employ small samples that researchers purposefully chose in order to discover new knowledge or to gain access to new or unfamiliar information. Exploratory research designs are widely used to discover more about a specific situation, event, or experience. Researchers use exploratory research designs when they know little about a topic, or where few prior definitions, few concepts, and little theory are available on a topic. For example, Bloom's (1980) content analysis sought to develop a comprehensive definition of prevention from the many different descriptions found in the interdisciplinary literature. Researchers call such a study exploratory because it seeks to develop a comprehensive definition where none was previously available.

Researchers use *descriptive designs* to provide information that details the character and quality of a sample or population. Descriptive designs are used to build upon the new terminology, definitions, concepts, and preliminary theory previously developed via exploratory research (Anastas, 1999). Descriptive research projects often use much larger and often more representative samples than those used in exploratory research. Researchers use larger sample sizes in content analyses to show the impact or spread of a social trend or characteristic. For example, Kramer, Pacourek, and Hovland-Scafe (2003) studied the end-of-life content in social work textbooks using a summary descriptive research design. Their comprehensive search for textbooks yielded a defined population of available texts at one point in time. Their cross-sectional design described the state of end-of-life content in social work textbooks at only one point in time. The study results described in detail the amount and type of end-of-life content found in contemporary social work textbooks.

Explanatory research designs are those that identify cause-and-effect relationships. Basic content analyses rarely use explanatory research designs. However, researchers may use them to distinguish groups of people on the basis of content of spoken or written communication. For example, Gottschalk and Gleser (1960) found that they could reliably distinguish real from fictitious suicide notes based solely on their content. Similarly, Gottschalk and Hoigard (1986) found that they could identify and distinguished minimally from more severely depressed groups of individuals on the basis of their written statements. In the depression study, the researchers instructed participants to write about specific life events and views in a short (under 500 words) statement. Once the researchers identified keywords to create a *dictionary* (listing) of search terms, computer software could then differentiate subgroups of people based on the content analysis of their written statements. Such content analyses may be very useful in developing and refining theories of depression or suicide for further research. Coupled with multivariate quantitative research techniques such as discriminate analysis, content analysis methods may be helpful in shaping explanatory research.

Data Reduction in Content Analysis

All content analysis is a form of data reduction. The U.S. Government Accounting Office (1996) states that content analysis is a method for sorting through large volumes of data in a systematic fashion. That is, many texts including hundreds of words and phrases are compressed into a few core categories, themes, or ideas. Massive amounts of data can be succinctly summarized using content analysis. Basic content analyses routinely report results in a summarized manner, highlighting key features found in a data set. Such empirically grounded summaries are valuable resources for advocacy and action. Of course, the quality of such summarized evidence is best when readers can quickly determine in detail how the researcher performed the data reduction and data analysis. Krippendorff (1980, 2013) and Weber (1990) have both emphasized that *all* content analyses should be systematic and replicable. Done well, this is a key strength of basic content analysis.

Concordances: Indexing Data Sets

Scholars, researchers, and the public use some basic content analysis techniques to index and sort through data sets more efficiently and effectively. This is a specific form of data reduction. Researchers doing linguistics or studies of religious documents use basic content analysis techniques to build a concordance of specific terms found in the target document(s). A *concordance* is an alphabetical list of the keywords used in a book or body of work. Concordances typically focus on specific, literal, word use. Yet most concordances also provide short phrases, putting the word in its immediate context for clarity. This contextualizing is known as "keyword in context," or KWIK in its abbreviated form. For example, there are online or print concordances for the Bible (Strong's Exhaustive Concordance, 2013), the Mishnah (Mieses, 1929), and the Koran (Kais, 2011). There are also print concordances of Shakespeare's complete works (Bartlett, 1969) and the lyrics to all of the Beatle's songs (Campbell & Murphy, 1980). Current content analysis software and generic qualitative data analysis software will also generate concordances from texts. Many software programs will also display keywords (search terms) in their textual contexts.

Note that a concordance adds detail to the information provided in a reference list or bibliography. In this way, concordances are a form of data reduction that can direct and focus future efforts. Concordances are efficient and very helpful for some research purposes. Before online resources were available, concordances allowed scholars and others to quickly locate selected keywords and passages. The work of basic content analysis—a thorough reading of the text and the literal coding of words or passages—fits smoothly with the creation of a concordance. Concordances reduce the effort that future researchers must expend to find specific text materials. However, a concordance is only of benefit if one's research purpose is to locate one or more passages that include a specific word or phrase in a text. This is most common in linguistic analyses and studies of a specific text or body of texts. Such work might show how the use of a term or phrase changes over time. Scholars might also use a concordance to explore how a specific author uses the same phrase to convey different—or the same—meanings in different works.

Use of concordances in social work research publication is extremely rare. Concordances are typically much too long to fit in the 20 typed-page format of most contemporary print journal articles. Nonetheless, Kramer and colleagues (2003) included a very complete listing of end-of-life content areas as an appendix to their basic content analysis of end-of life-content in social work textbooks. However, this thorough listing was not linked to specific texts and pages as in a true concordance. Still, it does provide a very helpful list of content areas and potential codes for future researchers. It thus focuses future research efforts and reduces the effort needed to find specific materials.

In social work, as shown in the examples provided earlier, researchers mainly use basic content analysis descriptively to show the proportion or percentage of manifest content in an article, a book, or a number of related articles or books. Exploratory and descriptive research designs predominate in the social work literature. Basic content analysis provides a clear evidence base and methodology for grounding such judgments in transparent evidence. Readers can understand how the study was completed and understand the evidence upon which it is based. Basic content analyses provide a basis for taking stock of the state of discourse and can be a sound source for advocacy. This is the most common purpose for using content analysis research in social work.

SAMPLING IN BASIC CONTENT ANALYSIS

Sampling in content analysis is often multistage in nature. That is, the researchers initially select a specific set of texts or files, then within this material identify subunits of interest. From within the subset of relevant data, specific segments may be sampled as well. For example, in Lalayants, Tripodi, and Jung's (2009) study of international research, a sample of three journals with large circulations was initially selected. The researchers next chose a 10-year time period for the study, which allowed comparison of two 5-year-long time periods to show any change in the frequency of international research articles. Within these three journals, a subset of research articles, rather than conceptual or opinion pieces, was then identified by the researchers. A typology of three forms of international research was identified and used to distinguish appropriate content from the research articles identified within the three research journals. This typology included supranational, intranational, and transnational forms of international research. The researchers might have further limited their sample to the "Literature Review" or "Methods" sections of these articles as locations where relevant data might be found most often. Of course, an article's title, its introduction, and its problem statement might also provide sufficient information to identify the type of research used. Basic content analysts must define their samples with sufficient scope and detail to address their chosen research question, but often they can improve the efficiency and focus of their work by using a multistage sampling method. Sampling in content analysis is rarely a single-step endeavor.

Sampling Terminology

In basic content analysis, one may define the focus of the study in such a manner as to include an entire population or a selected sample taken from a larger population. That is, one can study *all* the articles written by a given author, a *population*, or one could take a smaller subset of all the articles, a *sample*. The approach chosen depends on the purposes of the research and the size or volume of the available data. To create an index or concordance of a set of documents, the full population of documents would need to be studied. All of the documents would be included, examined, and indexed. Such an approach can be called a *census* of the items studied since the study covers an entire population. Population-based studies tend to be expensive. The "membership" of the population may also change over time, for instance, when new documents are located or published.

One key technique for sampling from a defined population is to establish a *sampling frame*. For instance, to track the number of gay or lesbian characters in TV shows over time, a list of the all the networks or shows to be studied would be needed; such a comprehensive list is a sampling frame. The sampling frame would include all the shows available (the population) or some fraction of them (a sample)—say, the shows viewed by the greatest number of people. To track the amount and types of end-of-life care content found in social work textbooks, by contrast, a researcher might choose to identify and examine a carefully selected sample in great detail. This would reduce the expense of the study and take less time while still offering a portrait of content in the books included in the sample. However, in most instances, content analysts must generate their own sampling frames, as none that encompass relevant data may be immediately identifiable or available.

Issues in Basic Content Analysis Sampling

Krippendorff (2013) has pointed out that the sampled units in content analyses, such as texts or interviews, are not necessarily individual and independent. Selected works may reference each other or represent different editions or presentations of the same material. Books may be made into screenplays or movies, or parts of their soundtracks into popular music tracks. This means that one of the core assumptions of probability sampling—the independence of units—may be violated. Determining such interconnections of sampled units may not be possible, however, until an initial analysis of the data is completed. Yet for the appropriate use of some statistics, independence among the sampled units is required.

Further, not all texts may prove to be relevant and meaningful for a specific content analysis. Depending on the researcher's purposes, it may be appropriate to discard texts that are not revealing and to focus instead on only those that contain relevant materials. The units of interest to the researcher, such as LGBT characters in television shows, may be (sub)units within larger texts. It may not always be ideal or even feasible to use a probability sampling approach in content analyses. Equal probability of selection for each unit may be secondary to identification and selection of the most informative units. Thus, a more purposive sampling approach may be more appropriate for even basic content analyses of large data sets. Such a method gives up equal probability of selection in favor of greater relevance and efficiency.

Sampling in basic content analysis is frequently *purposive* or *theoretical* in nature. That is, researchers make sampling decisions to obtain the most informative and appropriate sample for the study's purposes. Yet in basic content analysis, many researchers use probability samples of large data sets. *Probability samples* are those in which each "case" (text or story) has an equal chance of selection. Probability samples allow use of inferential statistics to make generalizations about the population from which the sample was drawn. Based on probability theory, inferential statistics offer a set of rules for making quantitative data–based decisions. By contrast, nonprobability samples do not insure equal probability of selection but emphasize inclusion of content that is known to be representative, maximally different, or unique. The use of probability samples in basic content analysis is consistent with the positivist epistemology that usually serves as the foundation of such research. When rigorously applied, probability samples allow researchers to generalize from the sample they studied to the larger population from which the sample was drawn. For some basic content analyses, probability samples are appropriate and serve to limit researcher costs. Probability samples are also widely understood by readers.

Sampling in basic content analysis is often determined and "fixed" at the start of the research project. This fixed, one-time sampling method contrasts with research using "flexible" sampling methods (Anastas, 1999). In flexible methods, researchers create a cycle of sampling, data collection, and data analysis in which new findings suggest revisions in the sampling plan and data to be studied. Such sampling plans are appropriate to many forms of qualitative research, such as grounded theory. By contrast, basic content analyses tend to employ fixed sampling methods.

Sampling Subsets of Data

Because the data for content analyses are typically existing texts, the first choice a researcher must make is what material to include in the study—and when to stop. The researcher must decide what population to study. Such choices are often shaped by the research question in combination with prior research and theory on the topic. If the population is large, a probability sample may be a fine way to reduce costs, aid practicality, and keep a clear connection back to generalizations about the entire population. A range of dates may be set to focus on a specific issue (such as changes in accreditation standards occurring at 8-year intervals) or simply to limit the volume of data the researchers must examine. Such multistage sampling techniques seek to identify transparently the most relevant data to address the research question.

In the social work exemplars of basic content analysis described earlier, the researchers chose nonprobability sampling plans. One chose to study all the relevant research articles published over 10 years in three large-circulation social work research journals. Another study examined 1 year of dissertation content; yet another, 1 year of research course syllabi. These are practical sampling plans that produced relevant, compelling, and useful data. Yet whether or not the data are representative of all social work research journals, or dissertations or research syllabi, over many years, is not at all clear. Nonprobability sampling plans may be useful for advocacy but have limitations in terms of making formal generalizations about larger populations. But if one's research purpose is describe publications from the past year only, the nonprobability sampling plan may be quite sufficient.

Sampling and Statistics

Basic content analysts routinely use statistical tests to analyze their data. Statistical tests fall broadly into parametric and nonparametric types. *Parametric statistics* (such as the *t*- test, ANOVA, and regression) are predicated on assumptions that (a) the sample is representative of the population from which it is drawn, and (b) the sample is large enough to conform to the limiting distribution(s) of the selected test. These assumptions must be met to appropriately apply *parametric statistics*: those that require specific distributions for use (Randolph & Myers, 2013). To use parametric statistics appropriately, researchers must have probability samples and variables that meet the required levels of measure for each statistic. Content analysts who chose to use such parametric statistics should use probability sampling methods.

Given that probability samples may not be feasible or appropriate for some content analyses, the alternative is for researchers to use nonparametric statistics. *Nonparametric statistics* (such as chi-square and Mann-Whitney U) are those that rely on a particular distribution for their appropriate use. They are also appropriate to use with the nominal and ordinal level data that are common in basic content analysis.

"UNITIZING" THE DATA: THE CONNECTION OF SAMPLING AND CODING

While basic content analysis most often draws upon existing data, there are still many choices for the researcher to make (Weber, 1990). In addition to defining the overall sample, researchers must often make additional decisions about defining smaller "units" of data. Unitizing the data links the sampling and the coding processes. *Sampling units* are defined sections of a larger text used to make it more manageable. For example, in a content analysis of course syllabi, there are subsections of an entire syllabus such as "course description," "course objectives," and "required readings." Researchers may analyze each of these sections separately as distinct sampling units. In less structured texts, sampling units may be pages, paragraphs, or numbered sections. Researchers may use these natural sections to help organize their comparison of many similar documents. Sampling units should be determined in a manner that makes clear to the reader how they are useful in focusing the content analysis.

Recording units is the term used by content analysts to identify a specific meaningful passage of text or other material (Weber, 1990). Recording units are also known as "passages" of text or "quotations." Where texts lack defined sections, or content is found in many separate locations, recording units may not be easy to identify before detailed analysis of the data set is started. The researchers identify recording units because these passages or segments of data convey specific meanings of interest. For example, a sentence in the course objectives section of a graduate social policy syllabus states that the course will address diversity issues. The sampling unit is the course objectives section of the syllabus. The recording unit, chosen by the researcher, might be a sentence on diversity or a specific course objective. The recording unit might alternatively be a short phrase in a sentence covering multiple course objectives, or even a single word.

The label assigned to a recording unit, or passage of text, is a *code name* (Weber, 1990). The code name helps identify the content found in the recording unit, such as "diversity content." Later in the analysis, the number of times diversity content has been found and coded can be used to describe this content's prevalence in the syllabus, or even its relative importance compared to other content. Note, too, that code names may also serve as the basis for indexing selected content within a group of texts to help future researchers find the content quickly and efficiently. In Wyatt's (2012) study, meaningful passages were those parts of television programs in which a character was identified as explicitly gay, lesbian, bisexual, or transgender. To detail the evidence on which he based his conclusions, Wyatt could further identify the specific recording units in which the characters acted in a manner that articulated a specific sexual orientation. The type of sexual orientation (gay, lesbian, heterosexual, etc.) is the code name used to summarize the information found in the recording unit.

Note that the process of coding recording units is often complex. Even in basic content analyses, many interpretive decisions are required of the researchers. For instance, Wyatt (2012) does not make fully clear how he determined sexual orientation. He states that "to be listed a character should have appeared in *at least three episodes* and be *explicitly* gay, lesbian, bisexual or transgendered" [emphasis in the original]. Yet what qualifies as "explicitly" is not defined and is subject to some ambiguity. Direct verbal statements by the character or overt actions in the programs appear to be required, but this is not stated. Further, the title of Wyatt's study does not specifically include transgender characters while the criteria for listing does, and some shows also include transgender characters. This inconsistency occurred because no transgender characters were found until the late 1990s. At this time, Wyatt had been doing the study for many years.

Unobtrusive Data Collection—Minimizing Reactivity

Most basic content analyses use data that are obtained unobtrusively compared to in-person interviews. Data are typically publicly available documents or artifacts created for purposes other than research. Neither the creator of the message nor its intended receiver is necessarily aware the content is being analyzed (Weber, 1990). This reduces reactivity threats to the internal validity of content analyses, as the creators of the data are not likely to shape their work for an unknown audience. In contrast, participants in research interviews may well give a socially appropriate answer even if it doesn't reflect their own views and actions. Threats to internal validity are features of the research, which may undermine the meaningfulness of the results. Examples include reactivity to the researcher or the content in a research question, variations in responses brought about by asking the question in different words, or asking questions in a different order. These are not likely to be major issues when the data are originally generated for purposes other than research.

Yet there are a few basic content analysis projects that involve newly collected data. Both Gottschalk (1995) and Oxman et al. (1988) examined differences in language usage between people who have serious mental illness and those who do not. In this research, the data were brief statements in which participants were asked to describe their experiences, family, and social interactions. It is plausible that persons in distress might react to an interviewer with anxiety or with caution. Creating a written statement on one's own or using existing texts removes or reduces one threat to the validity of the data used in the study. When researchers use existing texts in basic content analyses, researcher reactivity is minimized.

Based on one's research purposes, audience, and the nature of the data, researchers must choose between more basic content analysis models and more interpretive ones. There are both assets and liabilities to any such decision, thus great care is required.

CODING IN BASIC CONTENT ANALYSIS

Basic content analysis may use either deductive, a priori coding, or inductive coding techniques, or a mix of both techniques. In basic content analysis, deductive coding lists, also called *dictionaries*, are widely used. Researchers develop a priori codes before the analysis begins. Such lists are generated deductively from previous work and theory. For example, codes applied to teenagers' descriptions of activities that might pose risk of HIV infection could be coded using a set of codes that covers what is known about established infection vectors. Epidemiological researchers often use such a priori codes where risks or other factors of interest are well known from previous research.

Researchers use inductively generated codes when there is no well-established set of applicable codes, or where such existing codes or theory are viewed as limited. Even the best deductively generated codes often prove to be limited in real-world application. Thus, identification of new, inductively defined codes is often part of basic content analyses. Researchers inductively develop such codes through a detailed analysis of the collected data set.

Haney, Russell, Gulek, and Fierros (1998) describe a typical approach to inductive or emergent coding. First, two or more people independently review the same materials and develop a set of working codes that cover the content well. Second, the researchers compare their lists of codes and reconcile any differences that appear. Often, after discussion, some codes applied by only one researcher are retained as relevant; still other codes are consolidated, collapsed, or eliminated. This process simultaneously refines the code list and trains the researchers to improve reliability of coding. At the end of this step, the research team finalizes a consolidated code list. Third, the researchers use the consolidated checklist to independently apply codes to the remaining data. Finally, the researchers again check the reliability of their completed coding.

By convention, researchers seek high levels of inter-coder agreement (LeBreton & Senter, 2008). The most common measure used is simply a percentage of agreement (Stolarova, Wolf, Rinker, & Brielmann, 2014). Where the codes have more than two values or categories, researchers may also use a Cohen's kappa statistic. By convention, kappa values of .61 or higher establish substantial reliability (Viera & Garrett, 2005). If the researchers do not obtain at least this level of kappa result, the researchers repeat the coding and review process until such levels of agreement are obtained. The kappa statistic is affected by the relative prevalence of values, which may require careful interpretation of results (Krippendorff, 2013).

Doing the Coding

Once a preliminary set of codes is generated, the researchers compare their results, discuss areas of agreement and difference, and revise the code list. The discussion may also generate ideas not found in the preliminary code list but that the researchers think should be looked for as data collection and analysis continues. New, inductively generated codes may also be added to include meaningful text passages that did not fit within the original deductively generated code list. The result is a code list or "dictionary" all the coders will use to analyze the data. At the same time, coders need to stay open to innovations or unique instances in the materials that may not fit easily within the code list. These instances should be brought to the full team for consideration.

Coding categories may be either broad or narrow depending on the researcher's purposes. Narrow categories may be found to have few instances in the data. Broad categories may have many instances in the data. Broad categories may also be revealed to consist of several components—such as specific medical and mental health diagnoses within a broad category like "types of illnesses." Whether broad or narrow, categories must be optimal for meeting the researcher's purposes and answering the research question. A breakdown by diagnosis may be more helpful if the goal is to provide guidance to care providers from different professions. A broader category may be sufficient to establish the overall incidence of such concerns.

Challenges in Coding

Coding is a difficult process that requires concentration, creativity, and self-reflection by the researcher. Beyond being labor-intensive, coding is also a time-consuming process. Identifying meaningful recording units requires strong familiarity with the materials under study and multiple reviews of the material. In many instances, definition of the coding categories requires careful thinking and refinement. For example, in Wyatt's study of television characters, he sought to study only "regular or recurring" characters. He decided that in order to be counted, "a character should have appeared in at least three episodes." Similarly, determining that the characters are gay, lesbian, bisexual or transgender also required a clear definition. Where there was no explicit statement of sexual orientation by the character, Wyatt (2012, paragraph 2) decided that "effeminate (but not gay) male characters, mannish (but not lesbian) female characters, and gender-shifting science fiction characters are generally not listed." In other words, sexual orientation had to be quite overtly stated or overtly established to be included. It also had to be consistent across the three or more episodes in which the character appeared. This use of manifest content is typical of basic content analysis. Both creating codes and applying them can be challenging.

Validity and Reliability in Coding

Validation is the demonstration of evidence in support of the appropriateness of the inferences made in a study or report. To Polkinghorne (1988), validity of an analysis or a theory refers to results that have the appearance of truth or reality. This may also be called credibility or persuasiveness. A study is said to be *valid* if its measures actually measure what they claim to measure and if there are no logical errors in drawing conclusions from the data. In content analysis, the "measures" are usually researcher-generated coded categories that capture the meaning of the material under study. Such categories and coding schemes are usually not standardized but specific to the research project and its purposes.

The validity of basic content analyses appears to be assumed by most authors. Since the data are most often described in detail using well-established methods, validity is not questioned. Indeed, most content analysis coding systems are *face valid* in that the data appear to fit well with the interpretations made of them. The data are presented in some detail to the reader and may be very familiar to some readers. Further efforts to establish the validity of an analysis are rare in published basic content analysis reports. Yet to some statisticians and quantitative researchers, such face validity is a limited type of validity, as it does not involve cross-comparison with other measures. On the other hand, the degree of inference made in basic content analysis is often so literal and manifest that cross-comparison is not deemed necessary. The codes, and their ties to the original evidence, must be transparent and appear both clear and compelling to the reader.

Another form of validity is content validity. *Content validity* is concerned with representativeness—that the content covered by the data and analysis is representative of the larger domain of knowledge, values, and skills of interest. In this vein, Cronbach and Meehl (1955) state that content validity is established by showing that the test items are a sample of a universe in which the investigator is interested. Similarly, the categories created for a content analysis should convincingly constitute a subset of subject matter found in the data and thus should display content validity.

Criterion validity, the correlation of one test or measure with another that covers the same topic, is rare in content analyses. This is because content analyses often target unique data sets and unique content. The lack of other studies of the same content often makes cross-comparisons of the yield of multiple studies impossible. However, the validation of the interpretative content analyses discussed by George (1959a) did involve the qualitative comparison of two types of data (interpretations of speeches and military actions) that affirmed the accuracy of his analysis. In this case, the correspondence between analyses of the different data types was used as the criterion for establishing the validity of the interpretative analysis.

Establishing Inter-rater Reliability

Reliability addresses the question of whether different researchers categorize the data in the same way. It also addresses the question of whether the same person generates consistent results over time and different data. Popping (2010, p. 1067) states that "the purpose of reliability assessment is to assure that a data-generating process can be replicated elsewhere, by other investigators, using the same coding instructions and the same text but different raters." Reliability checks are also used to assess the reproducibility of coding within a study: Do different researchers code the same data in the same way? While quantitative approaches to validity are infrequent in basic content analyses, quantitative estimates of reliability are quite common. Inter-rater consistency measures are of particular interest.

Many content analysts use established metrics of inter-rater reliability to summarize the quality of their joint coding work. Lombard, Snyder-Duch, and Bracken (2002) reported that 69% of the content analysis articles they examined included specific reliability assessments. An initial step is to establish the inter-rater or inter-coder reliability of the coding completed by two or more raters. If a high level of agreement among raters is found (80% or higher agreement or a Cohen's kappa statistic greater than .61), rating continues using this same code list. Note that coding the presence or absence of specific content tends to yield inter-rater reliability levels well over 95%, while coding with many categories or multiple levels of intensity yields inter-rater reliability levels of 80% or sometimes lower (Lombard et al., 2002). Subtle judgments may be more difficult for teams of coders to do uniformly, while identifying if specific content is present or not is less difficult.

Percentages of inter-rater agreement or statistics such as alpha or kappa can be calculated to quantify reliability. Different measures are used based on the nature of the coding, the number of coders, and the level of measure of the coded content. Formulas for these measures are available online or in statistics texts; statistical software (such as SPSS, Stata, or SAS) can readily calculate many of these statistics.

Cronbach's alpha is a measure of the *internal consistency* of coding based on inter-item correlation among the ratings (Cronbach, 1951). Alpha measures the extent to which codes assigned correlate highly with each other. An alpha value of .61 is considered adequate, while alpha values of .81 or greater are considered strong.

Another reliability statistic is Cohen's *kappa*, which is a measure of *inter-rater reliability* that establishes the degree of consensus or homogeneity between two raters of the same ordinal-level content. Landis and Koch (1977) state that a kappa value of .71 or higher is acceptable and values of .81 or higher are outstanding. For categorical (or nominal-level or dichotomous) data, consensus is measured as number of agreements divided by total number of observations.

Intraclass correlation (ICC) is used to measure inter-rater reliability for two or more raters on interval-level, continuous measures on small data sets ($n < 15$) (Shrout & Fleiss, 1979). Values of .71 or higher are acceptable and values of .81 or higher are outstanding, comparable to the appraisal of Cohen's kappa values. It may also be used to assess test-retest reliability. A *Pearson's r* correlation coefficient is used to measure inter-rater reliability for two or more raters on interval-level, continuous measures and larger sample sizes ($n \geq 15$).

Krippendorff (2013) offers an extensive review of statistics that may be used in basic content analysis. Popping (2010) describes three approaches to reliability assessment in content analysis and details the statistics used by each method to document reliability. Readers are referred to these excellent resources for further detailed statistical analysis information.

Both the concepts of validity and reliability reflect a positivist or realist epistemology in which data are assumed to be independent of the observer/coder and stable or unchanging over time. That is, coding by the same person on the same data should be stable and consistent over time. Other coders should be able to agree to a good degree on the adequacy of the original coding. At a later time, other researchers should also be able to replicate the coding results of the original researchers and raters using the same data.

Concerns about Validity and Reliability

In 2004, Cronbach reflected on the validity and utility of his Cronbach's alpha measure of reliability, stating, "I no longer regard the formula [for alpha] as the most appropriate way to examine most data" (2004, p. 403). While not refuting the use of the alpha statistic, Cronbach made several comments about establishing reliability. First, he noted that homogeneity of the content under study is important to establish by expert consensus, not solely by statistical methods. In content analysis, establishing the homogeneity of coded content can be difficult but is indeed important. Basic content analysis seeks to limit this problem through the use of literal codes. Cronbach (2004) also advocates that use of a coding scheme should be taken into account to make absolute decisions versus differential decisions when appraising reliability. In accordance with the views of Popping (2010), researchers may be better able to make consistent judgments about absolute differences (e.g., material is present or not) than on hierarchical rankings or more subtle distinctions.

Mislevy (2004) has questioned whether there can be any real reliability without indices of reliability. Applying hermeneutic techniques, Mislevy advocates that test makers and coders think carefully about the inferences they make. This is important, because conclusions often involve multiple arguments or chains of reasoning drawing upon massive amounts of evidence. He notes that standardized techniques such as statistics may fail if researchers quantify content they don't know much about. Mislevy argues that more complex assessments of reliability, using techniques drawn from cognitive psychology, may be more appropriate than statistical techniques.

Thompson, McCaughan, Cullum, Sheldon, and Raynor (2003) take a more constructivist view of reliability, stating it is not a property of a test or coding system but is an attribute attached to data and their interpretation. Thompson and colleagues find most tests and, by extension, most coding schemes unreliable. They emphasize careful review of reliability in all studies using standardized measures. Viewed this way, reliability is less about specific research methods or statistics and more about the communicative utility of a claim of reliability within a specific group of researchers or scholars. Claims of reliability must be credible within the understanding of the audience to which the claim is made, but may be found lacking by others who require a different basis for making such claims.

These critiques of reliability, including those of Cronbach, may be viewed as being linked to constructivist or interpretivist concerns about the limitations of positivist epistemology. That is, if one presumes there are multiple, different, and worthy views among people on social issues, techniques alone may not offer sufficient summary measures of reliability. Of course, social work scholars and researchers of good will thoughtfully differ on the importance of epistemology in research. What is notable is that the distinction between "basic" approaches and "interpretive" approaches is meaningful and important. Researchers must ensure that their work fits with their intended research purposes and the information needs and expectations—epistemological and otherwise—of their intended audiences.

DATA ANALYSIS IN BASIC CONTENT ANALYSIS

Where the research focus is on a specifically defined set of documents, many different analytic tools are applied in basic content analysis. A *word list* of all the words found in the documents can be generated manually or using computer software. *Word frequencies* detail how often specified words are found in the text documents. Note, too, that the omission or infrequent use of expected words may also be meaningful for some research purposes. As noted earlier, a *concordance* is an alphabetical index of all the words in a text or groups of texts that specifies every instance in which a specific word is used and the context in which it is used. The context may be a phrase or passage in which the word is embedded. Concordances of key terms in the Bible and other religious texts are commonly used to help scholars locate terms and to explore the contexts in which keywords are used. Researcher-defined keywords may then be sought in specific contexts, generating a list of quotations or passages showing *keywords in context*. While most content analyses examine texts, key elements may also be sought in the context of images or objects. For example, the use and placement of words in advertisements may have an impact on their meaning and emphasis for marketing purposes. Comparison of the locations of words across multiple advertising images could be correlated with its marketing impact.

Sometimes keywords are expected to be found only in certain contexts, so finding them outside of the expected context may stimulate one's thinking about why such an exception occurs. Thus *keywords out of context* are sometimes sought in order to stretch one's thinking and identify exceptional word usage. All of these word listings may be created manually or by using computer software.

Basic content analysis may be organized by formal research hypotheses. A *hypothesis* is a statement of a specific type of relationship between two or more variables. Hypotheses are usually based on deductions from theory prior to data collection or analysis. However, in many cases content analysis is used descriptively to document what is present or absent in specific texts or materials. For example, it may be a researcher's impression that very few images of persons of color appear in the pictures on waiting room walls in mental health clinics. To examine this idea, the researcher may count images of people found in mental health clinic waiting rooms. Coding criteria to distinguish people of color from white people must be established (and could be complex). A simple frequency count could be used to concretize the research findings. The researcher may begin the work with the formal hypothesis that fewer people of color are found in waiting room pictures than are white people. No formal hypothesis, however, is required for such descriptive statistical analysis. Yet a researcher might chose to apply a chi-square analysis to these results, in which case a more formal research hypothesis might be appropriate.

Data Analysis Using Descriptive Statistics

Appropriate use of statistics in content analysis first requires selection of statistics based on the level of measure of the coded data. Several options are available for the analysis of data in content analysis.

Levels of Measurement

Level of measurement refers to a hierarchy of types of data. *Measurement* is the process of assigning values, most often numbers, based on a specified rule or system. Stevens (1946) asserts that measures must have specific properties in order to be used appropriately in mathematical operations. For example, it makes no sense to add up "Methodists" and "Buddhists," but each coded category separately may be useful in classifying data. Stevens' level of measurement scale includes four types: nominal, ordinal, interval, and ratio.

Nominal-level measures include categories that are (a) mutually exclusive and (b) exhaustive to the content under study. While this sounds very technical, it means the categories may not overlap and must cover all the content the researcher intends to study.

Ordinal-level measures must define categories that are (a) mutually exclusive, (b) exhaustive to the content under study, and (c) have a rank order or hierarchy. For example, having completed some high school education reflects more education than only completing fifth grade. Note that the exact number of years of education a person has completed is not fully clear in an ordinal hierarchy.

Interval-level measures define categories that are (a) mutually exclusive, (b) exhaustive to the content under study, (c) have a rank order or hierarchy, and (d) have specific, equal units between values. For example, having completed 16 years of education is 10 years more than a person who has completed only 6 years of education. Categories (called values) are clear, a hierarchy of defined values exists, and the nature of the differences among the values is specified.

Finally, *ratio*-level measures define values that are (a) mutually exclusive, (b) exhaustive to the content under study, (c) have a rank order or hierarchy, (d) have specific, equal units between values, and (e) have a non-arbitrary zero point. Some measures have both positive and negative values around a zero point. For example, temperature in degrees may be positive or negative. In the Celsius temperature system, water freezes at zero degrees, which makes it a non-arbitrary standard. Temperatures may be higher or lower than zero degrees, and each unit (degree) represents a consistent difference in temperature.

Level of measurement is important because more mathematical operations can be performed on interval and ratio measures than can be performed on nominal or ordinal categories. There are more statistical methods to analyze interval- or ratio-level data than there are for nominal or ordinal data. Statistics used for quantitative analysis in content analysis are determined in large part by the level of measure of the coded data.

Frequencies and Correlations

The analysis of data in basic content analysis often centers on a quantitative analysis. Researchers use counts or frequencies of specific content or events to describe the data under study. For example, a researcher may find that only 20 of the 100 online therapy websites studied explicitly offer licensing information about the online therapist. Such data clearly describe and summarize the availability of licensing information found regarding online therapists.

Beyond frequencies, correlations among specific content may be calculated. For example, a researcher may find that the verb following an online therapist's name has positive connotations 90% of the time, is neutral 10% of the time, and is never negative. Such information can be very valuable in empirically supporting what may otherwise be seen as the researcher's subjective observation. For example, Kramer and colleagues (2003) sought to examine how much end-of-life care content was found in widely used social work textbooks. Content analysis provided a descriptive summary of how much content on end of life care was present in their sample social work textbooks. Their study also provided information on what specific end of life content is provided and in what contexts—in this case, in which courses. Researchers may also use basic content analysis to identify what materials are omitted from books and articles. Most basic content analyses in social work use descriptive statistics as their key data analysis technique.

Inferential Statistics

Researchers should bear in mind that inferential statistics can also be used to analyze data in basic content analyses. For example, Gottschalk (1995) hypothesized that a basic content analysis of word frequencies in personal narratives could distinguish persons who might warrant a psychiatric diagnosis from persons who did not. Indeed, word-use frequencies differed as hypothesized between the two groups. Clinical observations were used to further validate the results of the inferential statistical comparisons. Similarly, Oxman et al. (1988) used a basic content analysis to distinguish people fitting four different psychiatric diagnostic categories by the words they used most frequently. These researchers also found that word use differed among the four groups. In this case, discriminant function analysis could be applied to predict group membership among future participants.

The Gottschalk-Gleser scale (1969) was developed by combining expert human judgments and factor analyses of human verbal behavior. This content analysis–based screening tool serves to differentiate a number of psychiatric traits and rank them for intensity.

Inferential statistics may be used to both test hypothesized group differences, and test hypothesized associations among variables. Researchers must take care to meet the limiting assumptions of such statistics, which may require probability samples, homogeneity of variance/covariance, and multivariate normality. Samples sizes should be determined using power analyses (Dattalo, 2008).

RESEARCHER REFLECTION AND REFLEXIVITY

While researcher self-reflection and reflexivity are not disallowed in basic content analysis, they are very rarely mentioned in publications. Neither texts on methods nor published studies include self-reflection as a key part of basic content analysis. This is consistent with a positivist or realist epistemological stance, in which researchers emphasize objectivity and adopt a distant observer stance. The appropriate and complete use of high-quality research methods is presumed to generate objectivity and rigor.

The main limitations of this stance are that researchers may minimize attention to the larger contexts in which the research takes place and may fail to identify either conceptual limitations or personal biases. Of course, neither self-reflection nor broader reflexivity guarantees optimal identification of the limitations of any form of research, yet they can be helpful. Basic content analysts may choose to include self-reflection and reflexivity in their projects and publications. Such review is common in qualitative research in which researchers seek to locate their work in context and to help the reader understand their potential biases in some detail.

CHAPTER SUMMARY

Basic content analysis is what most social workers and researchers from other disciplines think of as content analysis. It may be applied to existing texts or to newly collected, primary data. Basic content analysis is usually predicated on a positivist or realist epistemological base. It is most often used in descriptive research designs, but it can be used in exploratory, correlative, and explanatory research designs as well.

Coding of unstructured data involves methods drawing on qualitative research coding techniques, but is generally very literal and addresses manifest content. Basic content analyses are most often analyzed using statistical methods. Basic content analyses can provide useful evidence for scholarship and advocacy.

Chapter 3 will examine interpretive content analysis. This approach extends the core methods of basic content analysis to include, as the name implies, interpretative coding and analytic processes. Not only manifest content but also latent content is included in interpretive content analysis. Newly collected primary data are more common in interpretive content analyses than in basic content analyses. Interpretive, narrative-based data analyses are more common in interpretive content analysis, further distinguishing it from basic content analysis.

3

Interpretive Content Analysis

This chapter will examine interpretive content analysis. Following an introduction to interpretive content analysis, three exemplar studies will be analyzed in detail. This chapter on interpretive content analysis, as in Chapters 2 and 4, will explore content analysis using a standard outline. This structure will guide the reader in both planning a new study and reviewing completed studies. The components of interpretive content analysis include (1) the research purposes of content analysis, (2) target audiences, (3) epistemological issues, (4) ethical issues, (5) research designs, (6) sampling issues and methods, (7) collecting data, (8) coding methods, (9) data analysis, and (10) the role of researcher reflection. In combination, these 10 components can help researchers appraise the overall integrity and rigor of a content analysis proposal or of a completed project.

AN INTRODUCTION TO INTERPRETIVE CONTENT ANALYSIS

To date, researchers have rarely identified their use of interpretive content analysis in social work studies. As of March 2015, *Social Work Abstracts* showed only three publications citing the use of interpretive content analysis. Yet researchers can find many more interpretive content analyses in the larger databases used in psychology, nursing, education, and sociology.

There is, however, no simple dividing line between basic content analysis and interpretive content analysis. Some basic content analyses use inductive approaches to coding and may code latent material. As we shall see in the next chapter, there is also no clear diving line between interpretive content analysis and qualitative content analysis. Yet some methodologists of content analysis identify interpretive content analysis as a distinct research method.

We draw a heuristic distinction between basic content analysis and more interpretive approaches to content analysis. Basic content analyses, we have argued, are those that tend toward the use of deductively generated coding categories, use more literal or low inference in coding methods, and direct less attention to the contexts of communication and meaning making. They typically draw on quantitative statistical analytic methods. It also appears that basic content analysis draws on positivist or realist epistemologies. Basic content analyses are useful when they summarize or describe data or behavior effectively or when used to predict or explain relationships within the data.

In contrast, Krippendorff (2013, p. 24) defines what we label interpretive content analysis as "a research technique for making replicable and valid inferences from texts (or other meaningful matter) to the contexts of their use." Specific procedures are still required to ensure replicable and valid results, as well as to make claims about context. In interpretive content analysis, however, meaning is not simply "contained" in the text (p. 25). Interpretative content analysis, to Krippendorff, goes beyond descriptive questions of "what" and "how" and continues on to inferences about "why," "for whom," and "to what effect" (p. 27). It is neither merely literal nor necessarily solely descriptive in purpose (pp. 26–27). Researchers can address both the antecedents and the consequences of communication, allowing exploration of both the causes and effects of communication along with its explicit content. This helps researchers answer questions when direct access to original sources is limited or impossible, such as when the events are in the past or when participants are unavailable or deceased. Krippendorff (1980, p. 51) notes that much "content analysis research is motivated by the search for techniques to infer from symbolic data what would be either too costly, no longer possible, or too obtrusive by the use of other techniques." Baxter (1991, p. 240) notes that "if a researcher is interested in a richer understanding of the meanings of content, manifest content analysis will not be as enlightening as what I shall call interpretive content analysis."

Further, interpretive content analysis may go beyond a simple frequency-count approach to data analysis, providing data for abductive inferences from latent content. Indeed, Ahuvia (2001, p. 139) states that "interpretive content analysis is specially designed for latent content analysis, in which researchers go beyond quantifying the most straightforward denotative elements in a text." Interpretive content analyses may vary from coding and interpretations that stay very close to the explicit content of the data to others that require much greater contextual inference and specialized knowledge. Still, Krippendorff (2013) and other authors argue that interpretive content analysis must be firmly grounded in empirical data. Further, any interpretations must be justified through validating evidence.

Baxter (1991, p. 240) states that interpretive content analysis requires different methods from those used in basic content analysis. This is because "the act of interpretation potentially makes problematic the reliability with which the coders categorize units and the validity of resulting claims." Complete analysis of symbolic communication also requires attention to meaning, which may obligate attention to context. This focus on interpretation and meaning brings interpretive content analysis closer to the core techniques of qualitative research, particularly analytic induction (Bulmer, 1979) and abductive inference (Reichertz, 2014).

Some examples of interpretive content analysis will help illustrate the kinds of coding and analytic challenges faced by researchers using this method. They also show the more conceptually oriented interests of interpretive content analyses.

PUBLISHED EXAMPLES OF INTERPRETIVE CONTENT ANALYSIS

An Interpretive Content Analysis Defining Primary Prevention

While not specifically named as such, Bloom (1980) applied interpretative content analysis to developing an inclusive working definition of primary prevention in social work and closely allied fields. (Bloom's article is indexed as an interpretive content analysis in the *Social Work Abstracts* database.) He identified 24 "representative" definitions of primary prevention from the social science literature over a 20-year span of publications. Analysis of the shared content of these definitions yielded six codes. These codes fully reflected the core dimensions communicated by the original authors in Bloom's view. The dimensions are wide-ranging and offer some concepts regarding primary prevention that add context to the definition. He summarizes:

> Primary prevention ... involves planned actions (1) in selected biological-psychosocial-physical systems that are presumed to be causally linked to target events, (2) on a time dimension before some predicted untoward event (or some desired goal) has occurred, (3) directed toward reducing the incidence of the problem in a specific population of persons at risk, (4) such that the activities could obviate the negative events and promote the positive events, (5) using passive as well as active strategies as they seem appropriate, feasible, and ethical, and (6) with concomitant evaluation of the progress and outcome of such preventive efforts. (1980, Abstract)

That is, prevention acts on systems that are presumed to be the causes of specific events before they occur, to reduce risk and/or promote positive outcomes through specific actions, using appropriate and ethical strategies, ending with evaluation of the success of these efforts.

From a wide range of definitions, Bloom identified these six core components, leading to a general, conceptual definition of primary prevention. Note that the specific manifest elements are not solely Bloom's focus. Instead, a broadly applicable, conceptual, definition is sought, integrating many different viewpoints. Some readers may find this definition highly abstract and, perhaps, not particularly informative about the specifics of primary prevention. This would be a fair assessment, but it was not the purpose of Bloom's study. His goal was to create a general definition of the components of primary prevention that would fit multiple endeavors accurately. Interpretive content analysis can move beyond simple summation to generate conceptual ways of understanding data.

A critic might question if Bloom's (1980) sample of 24 representative definitions of primary prevention, even one selected from the social science literature over a 20-year span, was adequate for his research

purposes. Apparently, Bloom's sampling was informed by his wide reading in prevention, leading to a purposive sample of representative definitions. The sample is purposeful rather than probabilistic. The analysis
of the material is interpretive and summary, creating a synthesis of key
conceptual points. The analysis is not simply descriptive, nor does it
employ statistical methods. Researcher interpretations and syntheses
are employed at several points in Bloom's analysis, which results in a
clear and useful definition of primary prevention.

An Interpretive Content Analysis of Teaching Effectiveness

Another interpretive content analysis was used to build a model of effective teaching. Reagan (2010) used students' online evaluations of their
instructors to identify the attributes of effective teachers, with university institutional review board approval. Using 300 randomly selected
narrative evaluations from a "popular online faculty rating system,"
she identified from a wide variety of student comments six core themes
reflecting the attributes of effective teachers (p. iii). Reagan initially
identified each of these core themes using their relative frequencies,
though specific statistical data documenting the frequencies for each
theme were not included in the research report. Reagan (2010, p. 91)
states, for example, that "more than half of the 300 anecdotal comments
discussed the presence or absence of the 'Perceptive' attribution theme
in the classroom." Next, using interpretive content analysis, Reagan
"extended [her] thematic analysis of the students' comments by reartic-
ulating and interpreting the more *latent content*, defined by Berg (2008)
as the symbolism underlying the physically present data" (p. 93, emphasis in the original). That is, the six themes were not necessarily always
explicitly stated, but both Reagan and her second coder could clearly
infer them from the students' online comments. This created an audit
trail that Reagan used to show readers how she made the inferences in
her report.

Students' online evaluation comments included "Awesome teacher.
Freakishly smart. Helpful and his lectures are informative and he has
a good sense of humour. He'll challenge you and makes sure you learn
the material. He should teach other instructors in the program how to
teach" (Reagan, 2010, p. 80). Reagan interpreted this passage as "Student
is appreciative of instructor's knowledge and presentation, including

humour, with the goal of challenging the student to learn" (p. 80). She then coded this evaluation with the initial codes "Awesome," "Smart," "Humorous," "Helpful," "Informative," and "Challenging." Note that each of these codes represent manifest content in the data. Students, however, did not rate all instructors so positively. Another student's evaluation read, "Does not follow curriculum, inconsistent marker, hard to follow in class" (p. 80). Reagan interpreted this evaluation as meaning, "Student is dissatisfied with the absence of content, inconsistency in marking and lack of clarity in presenting the content" (p. 80). Note that "absence of content" is not manifestly stated in this student's evaluation. Reagan then coded this evaluation with the initial codes "Inconsistent" and "Unclear" (p. 80). Initial or preliminary codes are best when kept quite close to the specific content stated in each evaluation. Still, low-inference interpretations can focus on the meaning conveyed in the material even though they are not necessarily literal. For example, researchers may interpret sarcastic or ironic comments on the basis of their meaning rather than only their manifest content. Readers and other researchers might not always agree with the researcher's interpretations. In her content analysis, Reagan described her coding process transparently and in detail for reader review. The second step of combining and consolidating codes involves yet more interpretation. It also involves a move toward greater abstraction and categorization of the themes by the researchers.

Reagan (2010, p. 82) used a "qualified adult educator" as a second coder to establish the reliability of her codes and initial interruptions. This second coder questioned only eight of Reagan's interpretations (2.6%) (2010, p. 82). Percentage agreement was used to establish the reliability of the coding. Disagreements were resolved through discussion. Further, she established the trustworthiness of her interpretations by showing the reader that they were not superficial, biased, or insubstantial. By showing *how* the interpretive coding and analysis process was completed the author also established her credibility with the reader.

Across the 300 evaluation's, Reagan (2010) identified six overarching themes. The six attributes of effective teachers were that they were (1) articulate, (2) competent, (3) content experts, (4) empowering, (5) perceptive, and (6) trustworthy. These themes are both descriptive and conceptual in nature, including abstract, latent content as well as manifest content.

After generating these themes from the data, Reagan compared them to the prior research on the attributes of effective teachers. From these codes, Reagan created the ACCEPT model of Student Discernment of Effective Teaching Characteristics. This model provides a methodology for using informal faculty evaluations to promote excellent teaching practices. It may make faculty evaluations more flexible and ultimately lead to improved teaching and learning.

Reagan's study employed a random sampling method, coupled with interpretive coding. Her analysis drew from ideas present in the prior literature, yet each code was inductively supported by content found in the participant's comments about their teachers. The coding was therefore both deductive and inductive in design. Reagan did not identify and discuss potentially disconfirming comments in the study. Face validity was sought, and several traditional techniques were used to enhance the reliability of the coding and data analysis.

An Interpretive Content Analysis of African-American Pregnancy Loss and Infant Mortality

In a third example, Barnes (2008) examined the perspectives of African-American women on pregnancy loss and infant mortality. Given that more than twice as many African-American as white infants die annually in the United States, she sought to explore how women understand this difference. Thirteen African-American women from Virginia participated in a focus group or in individual interviews. Ten of these women had been pregnant and three had experienced a pregnancy loss. After obtaining informed consent, the data collection addressed factors that participants' viewed as leading to the higher mortality rate among African Americans, their pregnancy experiences, and their sources of support. Inductive content analysis after Berg (1995) and interpretive analysis after Benner (1994) "were used to develop categories, coding frames, paradigm cases, themes and vignettes from the data" (Barnes, 2008, p. 296). The article included several lengthy vignettes as the database for establishing several core themes.

For example, one interpretive theme reflecting the participants' views was that "racism does exist in the medical system" (p. 299). Barnes states that "one participant noted that perceptions of African-American women held by providers influence the care they provide and fosters a two-tiered system of medical care" (p. 299). The participant said:

> Well it could apply to prenatal care we get . . . maybe our medical providers have different expectations, so maybe we are not given the full benefit of certain treatments and information. I know for many black people treatments are imposed on them without knowing what questions to ask . . . treatments and withholding treatments. Maybe the differential expectations impact the kind of care that they give to us. It's hard to define racism because you can go to a doctor and he can find a problem and choose to treat what he wants to treat and can say I did not know that problem existed, when he did know that it existed. But he is the doctor, he is doing your internal exam, he can see it, but you can't see it so you very well don't know it and he can say I did not treat it because I did not think it was necessary. (Barnes, 2008, pp. 299–300)

Barnes interprets that

> Participants felt that doctors can select what patient conditions they will treat and that their selections can be grounded in subtle racist beliefs that are hard to define or detect. An example observed by one participant was the withholding of information on reproductive options from infertile women who were African American and poor. (p. 300)

Barnes also states that the views of these women "correspond with findings from several recent studies" (p. 302).

Barnes chose to illustrate each theme with a single interpretive example or paradigmatic case. It is not clear that any single example reflects the views of all or most of the participants, but each example is clear, vivid, and compelling. Coding and analysis are not literal, but are arguable low-inference interpretations. Context and latent content are used in developing the analytic themes. Note that a statistical frequency count was not used as an analytic technique. Barnes draws on the views of a small group of women to illustrate, and to interpret, the likely views of a much larger population of women. The overall purpose and focus of the research is descriptive. Barnes (2008, p. 303) clearly states that the study should not be generalized to all African-American women and that a larger sample with more socioeconomic status variation might have revealed different or more varied views than those from this sample.

Implications for practice stay close to the reported findings, suggesting that African-American women need social support, counseling, and education in the areas of pregnancy, stress management, and infant care. The importance of social workers' contextual knowledge of African-American history and lived experience was emphasized, along with the use of informal community supports in health and maternity care among this population. The implications for practice are low-inference interpretations, supported by the reported case material.

In summary, interpretative approaches to content analysis are those that go beyond literal codes based on manifest content alone. They draw on researcher interpretations and insights to generate codes and create analytic categories or themes. Coding is typically inductive, drawing on the study data set, contexts, and latent as well as manifest communications. Codes may be connotative in nature, rather than simply mirroring the original data. Connotative codes are those that "draw from the latent content [and] are arrived at by combining individual elements in a text to understand the meaning of the whole" (Ahuvia, 2001, p. 142). Researchers doing interpretive content analyses must nonetheless make clear to their readers how each code is grounded in the data or texts. Such efforts establish the validity of the codes and analysis. Traditional approaches to ensuring reliability in coding are commonly used, despite the interpretive nature of coding and analysis.

RESEARCH PURPOSES OF INTERPRETIVE CONTENT ANALYSIS

Researchers may use interpretive content analysis to describe content and meanings, to summarize large data sets, and to make inferences about intentions, thoughts, and feelings based on speech or other forms of communication. Interpretive content analysis might assess people's reactions to policies or services in order to identify those that are clear and appealing from those that are not (Ginger, 2006). With more interpretive and more contextualized inferences, researchers and data analysts can use content analysis to make judgments about intentions, needs, and potential actions. For example, interpretive content analysis was used during World War II to determine enemy intentions from study of the content of propaganda and known actions (de Sola Pool, 1960). One might assume that interpretive approaches to content analysis could be used currently to make inferences about the motives, purposes, and actions of terrorist groups. In such cases, the researchers would make informed inferences based on both manifest and latent content in context. Information may often be partial or incomplete, or its completeness may be impossible to assess with confidence. The original communicators may make purposeful distortions. Such interpretive content analyses do not rely solely on frequency counts of words or images. Instead, they require carefully informed, contextualized, and data-grounded inferences about the likely inner thoughts, purposes, and views of others that are not explicitly communicated (Ginger, 2006).

While most research designs used in interpretive content analysis are descriptive, it is important to note that they may also be used to make predictions and to test theories. If an interpretive content analysis suggests likely terrorist targets or plans, the accuracy of actions based on the analysis may be viewed as real-world tests of predictions or theories. However, such predictions tend not to address entire populations, but rather specific subgroups of individuals. Context is often a crucial factor shaping the usefulness of interpretive content analyses.

TARGET AUDIENCES FOR INTERPRETIVE CONTENT ANALYSIS

Interpretive content analyses are found in the literatures of many disciplines and professions. They are widely used in medicine, education, marketing, journalism, linguistics, communications, computer science, studies of literature, ethical studies, and religious studies. They are also used by spies and national governments to assess the intentions of other governments (de Sola Pool, 1960; George, 1959a). Researchers do not often state in their publications the distinction between basic and interpretive content analyses, made here heuristically.

Audiences for interpretive content analyses include the general public, users of specific services, advocacy groups, service providers, marketers, program and policy planners, business people, policymakers, and legislators. Interpretive content analysis may be used to inform, describe, evaluate, and summarize, as well as to provide a basis for advocacy and action.

The target audiences for interpretive content analysis also include other academics and professionals. Publications such as Barnes's (2008) describe the views of a group and to serve as preliminary guides to understanding and intervention. Such reports also raise awareness of understudied populations and begin development of concepts and theories for further research. Bloom's report illustrates how interpretive content analyses can be used to develop and refine concepts and theory.

EPISTEMOLOGICAL FOUNDATIONS OF INTERPRETIVE CONTENT ANALYSIS

As previously noted, there is little explicit discussion of epistemology in the content analysis literature as a whole. Krippendorff (2004, 2013) implies that a constructivist or interpretivist epistemological foundation may be used in interpretive content analyses. That is, if basic content analysts view meaning as contained within the words they examine, the meaning of words is self-evident and not subject to interpretation. Yet, more interpretative content analysts take the position that the researcher's purpose and frame of reference may make an important difference in the understanding of words in context. From this epistemological perspective, texts do not simply *contain* meaning but are instead *rendered meaningful by the perspective and understanding of the reader* for specific purposes. Readers may interpret and make meaning of the presented content from different standpoints, or from cultural backgrounds with very different purposes than those of the content analyst. This appears to be a constructivist epistemological position.

For example, (George, 1959a, 1959b) has claimed that interpretive content analyses of propaganda during World War II gave important information to Allied commanders. In analyzing speeches by Nazi leaders, interpretative content analysts were able to infer when new weapons would be deployed or delayed and identify changes within the Nazi leadership. Note that these speeches were intended by the

Nazi leaders to encourage support for Nazi war efforts and to wear down the will of the enemy. However, the interpretive content analysts interpreted the same speeches for very different purposes. The researchers sought to infer the likely actions and concerns of the enemy from the content of their propaganda. Such use of the propaganda data requires an inferential process that does not involve a literal match with the data. This illustration supports Krippendorff's (2013) position that meaning is not simply contained in words and images but can be interpreted by others with their own interests for their own goals.

While there is little overt discussion of the epistemology of content analysis in the literature generally, Krippendorff (2004, 2013) here appears to be taking a constructivist epistemological stance. This is in marked contrast to the positivist stance implicit in the work of the basic content analysts. At the same time, Krippendorff (2004, 2013) emphasizes that interpretations should be validated by comparing them to other types of data. For example, an interpretive content analyst's understanding of propaganda should be compared to actual events (even though these events may occur after the analysis). If the interpretation and the actions are found to be consistent, then the interpretation was essentially correct. The correspondence between interpretation and other evidence establishes the validity of the analysis in a traditional positivist manner. In this case, the content analysts' interpretations were demonstrated to be correct through enemy actions and were further validated by Nazi documents found after the war that affirmed their accuracy.

Critical or critical theory perspectives are rarely found in interpretive content analyses. While the research questions guiding content analysis may seek to describe the lack of specific content or perspectives in texts, the methods used by interpretive content analysts generally take a value-neutral perspective. Rather than actively emphasizing the interests or perspectives of a given group, content analysts use the method more descriptively than critically. This evidence may then be used abductively to advocate for a given purpose or position, but the data are typically treated as neutral in themselves. As interpretive content analyses become more common, critical perspectives on content analysis may emerge.

ETHICAL ISSUES IN INTERPRETIVE CONTENT ANALYSIS

Given prior harms to human research participants done by well-intended researchers, it is always wise and ethically sound to seek a formal institutional review before undertaking any research involving people. Ethics review regulations in the United States allow institutional review boards to determine that studies are exempt from review where risks are no greater than everyday hazards, to allow an expedited review where risks are slight, or to require a full review where risks that are more serious. Researchers doing any form of content analysis should seek review of their projects by an authorized ethics review board.

Readers will find a more complete discussion of ethical issues pertinent to both basic and interpretive content analysis in Chapter 2. A summary of ethical concerns specific to interpretive content analysis is offered here.

Interpretive content analysis may draw on either existing texts, newly collected data, or both. Where existing data are used exclusively in interpretive content analysis, studies may be exempt from formal review by an institutional ethics panel. The institutional review board, however, must make this determination. Some interpretive content analyses, such as the Barnes (2008) exemplar cited earlier, involve the collection of new data from human research participants via interviews. Such projects will always require formal institutional ethics review to protect human research participants.

As described more fully in Chapter 2, use of electronic data sources is an evolving area in research ethics. While such data are publicly available, contributors may not view their posting and textual materials as truly public. Researchers should consult with their institutional research ethics review board when using such data sources in content analyses of all kinds.

In the examples discussed earlier, both the Reagan (2010) and Barnes (2008) interpretive content analysis publications included brief statements that their studies had been reviewed by an institutional review board and approved by the board. Reagan (2012, p. 75) states that her study using online data was given a "waiver from full ethical review of research involving human participants based on this research being limited to secondary analysis of anonymized data." This was the formal determination that followed her application for institutional ethics review. Barnes (2008, p. 296) notes that "consent forms were read and signed by participants before beginning the focus group or interviews." This implies, but does not clearly document, that an institutional review was completed. Bloom (1980), whose data source was concepts in publications within the published academic literature, did not include human research participants. Bloom's study did not need an intuitional ethics review. Social work researchers are always advised to seek formal institutional review of any research project involving human participants directly or indirectly.

RESEARCH DESIGNS IN INTERPRETIVE CONTENT ANALYSIS

Most interpretive content analyses are descriptive in design. That is, they are used to describe and summarize the views found in texts or stated by research participants. The publications of Bloom (1980) and Reagan (2010) employ descriptive research designs. Still, interpretive content analysis may also be used as an exploratory research design, identifying new views, experiences, and needs. Barnes's (2008) interpretive content analysis blended both exploratory and descriptive design elements. (A complete description of research design types and their differences is found in Chapter 2.)

George's (1959a) analysis of Nazi propaganda shows that interpretive content analysis may also be used predictively, drawing on a contextual understanding of events. Interpretive content analyses using such designs, however, are rare in the social science literature. Descriptive designs predominate in this limited literature.

SAMPLING IN INTERPRETIVE CONTENT ANALYSIS

Sampling in interpretive content analysis appears to be mainly a single-stage process. Researchers initially identify a specific set of texts or participants, then seek out a subset of this initial sampling frame. Such samples are selected using either probability or purposive sampling techniques. (Sampling terminology is fully described in Chapter Two.) Reagan (2010) used a random (probability) sampling technique to identify the evaluations of teachers she would review. This technique provided an equal chance of selection for all teachers evaluated in the larger sampling frame. While Reagan notes that her coded themes were determined by the frequency of relevant content, it is not clear that the full study analysis is consistent with quantitative/statistical methods that would allow generalization back to the original population as a whole. This key strength of a probability sample does not seem to be used optimally in her study.

In contrast, Barnes (2008) used a purposive sampling technique to identify the African-American women who participated in her study. The participants included women who had never been pregnant, mothers, and women with pregnancy losses, to provide varied perspectives on the research topic. Barnes' sample did not seek to be representative of all African-American women, which she states clearly in the publication. In this study, interpretive content analysis was used for exploratory and descriptive purposes, with generalization to others left uncertain. Readers would need to test if the descriptive concepts reported in this study could be applied validly to other samples and settings. Nonetheless, Barnes's study describes concerns that will sensitize other researchers and practitioners to issues of concern to African-American women and families.

Krippendorff (2013) notes that the sampled units in content analyses, such as texts or interviews, are not necessarily independent of each other. Researchers using interpretive content analyses with probability samples and using statistical analysis methods must take care to review the independence of sampled units. Failing to do so may violate the assumptions for the appropriate use of certain statistical techniques.

Sampling of subunits within a larger sample of texts, as found in basic content analysis studies, does not appear common in the interpretive content analysis literature. Further, iterative coding does not appear to be widely used to refine and revise iteratively study sampling or data collection techniques. Such iterative, or cyclical, revision of samples is frequently found in qualitative research.

Qualitative sampling terminology and methods are more fully detailed in Chapter 4. Sampling goals and methods appear similar in both interpretive and qualitative content analyses. Terminology and conceptualization, however, is more fully developed as it relates to qualitative content analysis.

DATA COLLECTION IN INTERPRETIVE CONTENT ANALYSIS

As the three exemplar studies illustrate, data collection in interpretive content analysis may draw on use of a set of exiting texts or on the collection of new interview data. Data collection methods must be consistent with the overall purposes of the research project. Both the study sampling plan and data collection methods must be varied enough to include a variety of viewpoints and potential meanings. Collecting relevant, informative, and varied data is central to the content analysis data collection process.

Interpretive content analysts must apply self-awareness and self-refection to their work. The validity/credibility and generalizability or transferability of study findings are shaped by sampling and data collections methods. Biases and omissions in the study data must also be avoided. Ideally, researchers should demonstrate efforts to include in their studies potentially disconfirming or elaborating data.

Bloom (1980) sought to identify the essential features of the concept of prevention. His work offers an excellent and clear working definition, including some description of definitions that were not incorporated. Barnes (2008) provides her readers with clear descriptions of "paradigmatic" views, using the participants' own words in lengthy passages. However, she does not provide her readers with alternate views (if any were stated), nor does she illustrate the variety in how these women presented their views. When interpretive content analysts seek to describe the views of large groups of people, seeking out potentially divergent views is important to establishing validity/credibility. *Showing* the reader that some variation in viewpoints or meanings is present and that some views predominate is vital in a descriptive study.

Data collection links sampling and coding in interpretive content analysis. Obtaining a range of data, and coding it carefully, is the first step of the data analysis process in interpretive content analysis.

CODING IN INTERPRETIVE CONTENT ANALYSIS

Interpretive content analysis includes attention to both manifest and latent content. It also draws much more attention to the contexts in which people make, convey, and receive communications. These contexts are often vital to coding latent and symbolic content, as well as to fully understanding and coding the meaning of manifest communications.

Coding in most interpretive content analyses starts inductively with the preliminary raw data. Such "emergent" coding contrasts with the a priori or deductively generated coding used in many basic content analyses. This distinction between the methods is somewhat flexible: In some studies, both inductively and deductively generated codes are used in combination. In interpretive content analyses, emergent codes are generated on the basis of content of the data and seek to closely reflect its meaning in context. However, greater latitude is allowed in the coding process for interpretation and the impact of the contexts of communications. As in basic content analysis, multiple coders are commonly used, and codes lists are developed and refined to ensure reliable/consistent coding by all involved raters.

Coding in interpretive content analysis is largely descriptive. Researchers identify and tag for future use content of relevance to the study question. Bloom (1980) coded key elements of definitions of prevention. Reagan (2010) coded key elements of effective teaching as described in student evaluations. Barnes (2008) coded key concerns of African-American women regarding infant mortality and related medical care.

Interpretive content analysis allows for the use of connotative categories in the coding process and in the analysis of results. *Connotative codes* are those based not on explicit words but on the overall or symbolic meaning of phrases or passages. Connotative codes may be obvious to readers, or they may take some explaining by the researchers. Connotative codes should be clear and comprehensible, but they may be assigned on the basis of the researcher's specialized knowledge, or the details of a specific context. In such cases, the researcher must describe in detail for the reader how and why the connotative codes were assigned. In published articles, researchers typically provide their readers with examples of the coding process as illustrations of how the coding process was undertaken and justified.

Such connotative coding challenges are common in other inductive approaches to qualitative research methods such as grounded theory and ethnography. Glaser (1978) notes that connotative coding cannot follow a series of preplanned, deductively generated coding rules. He notes that coders may need considerable training or theoretical sensitivity (Glaser & Strauss, 1967). That is, not everyone will be able to make expert-level inferences with equal skill. Finally, Glaser (1978) notes that collaborative approaches to interpretive coding are often more successful than independent judgments. Collaboration among experts improves identification of latent information and insures that the researcher states the basis or process for making the inference clearly to others. It is crucial that researchers clearly explain latent connotations so that the linkage between evidence and interpretation is made explicit and is shown to be well grounded in data. All connotative codes ultimately need to be demonstrated as valid and need to be applied reliably by groups of researchers or coders.

Coding in interpretive content analysis is typically researcher generated and is clearly linked to specific, reported study data. Codes are more often inductively generated than deductively created a priori.

Developing a Code List

Miles, Huberman, and Saldaña (2014) point out that coding may be directed to several different elements of texts depending on the researcher's purposes. Coding may be descriptive of content, processes, concepts, emotions, values, and even hypotheses. Bloom (1980) clearly addresses conceptual content related to aspects of prevention. Interpretive content analysis may focus on a wide range of manifest and latent content in the target texts.

To develop a code list, the researchers review some selected materials and develop a tentative list of topics they find revealing or useful. In interpretative content analysis, the data used to start the coding process may be the first few documents or interviews in the study. The coders' goal is to identify the most revealing, meaningful, or common material in a set of documents. For example, in a study about how to reduce HIV infection risks with teenagers, attention to their knowledge of how the virus is transmitted, what constitutes safe sex practices, and even details about safe sex techniques (i.e., how to correctly use a condom) are all known to be important. These topics would make sense to include in a deductively generated list of codes to use in a content analysis. On a less well-studied topic, creating codes can only follow collection of preliminary data. In such cases, inductive coding is preferable.

While it is possible for a single researcher to undertake an interpretive content analysis, the use of multiple coders is optimal. Multiple coders bring different perspectives and awareness to the data analysis process. Identifying and exploring such differences can be a great help in clarifying codes and enhancing completeness. Exploring different views can help improve the coding process and the validity or credibility of the project as a whole (Cohen & Crabtree, 2008; Drisko, 1997, 2013b). Multiple coders also enhance study replicability (Krippendorff, 2013).

Researchers who have a clear sense of their research purposes more easily find and maintain a useful focus during initial coding work. It is possible for coders with different backgrounds or perspectives to find very different content meaningful. In such cases, preliminary training to focus the initial coding, and ongoing discussion to make give voice to differences in perspective and coding decisions is very important. This makes further coding more efficient and productive.

Context and Coding

Some interpretive content analyses draw heavily on the context of communications. Contexts may be as simple and local as noting a sarcastic communication in which the actual meaning is the opposite of what is explicitly stated. Yet contexts may also include the purposes of the communicator or those of the recipient. Communications may be intentionally distorted or shaded to specific purposes. In interpretive content analyses, researchers look for the many ways in which context may shape meaning making and help to identify and illuminate such processes to their readers. For example, Barnes (2008) sought to make more widely known the views of African-American women regarding infant mortality. Her coding, and her analysis, included considerable attention to the context in which healthcare is understood by this community. Participants' voiced concern that their community was not given the highest quality of prenatal care and that women were not given full information about their healthcare options. In a larger context, these views were interpreted to reflect the historical oppression of African-American women and, in particular, the disparities in healthcare access, services, and choices. Understanding the communications and views of these women may have been limited without attention to context. This is a strength of the interpretive content analysis approach.

When context is included in interpretation, researchers should also seek to establish high levels of inter-coder reliability. That is, multiple coders must agree that the interpretation is warranted and is based on the available data. In turn, readers must be fully informed of how the researchers understood the impact of context on their coding and analysis. Further triangulation of sources and types of evidence are useful ways to establish the validity of researcher interpretations (Denzin, 1970). For instance, as noted earlier, both enemy actions and later enemy documents affirmed the validity of researcher interpretations made from Nazi propaganda during World War II (de Sola Pool, 1960).

DATA ANALYSIS IN INTERPRETIVE CONTENT ANALYSIS

While coding is the first step in data analysis, formal data summaries complete the process. Most data presentation in interpretive content analysis centers on descriptive narratives, or themes, summarizing the collected and coded data. For example, Barnes (2008) used lengthy case descriptions to inform readers of the participants' core views. Such narrative presentation is compelling and vital. It is also obviously close to the participants' own words and manner of self-expression. Narrative-summary presentations reduce the data and highlight chosen themes and ideas. They are an effective and efficient means of informing the reader.

Researchers using narrative summaries must be self-aware and self-reflective to avoid selection bias in the narratives they choose to include and to exclude. The art of data analysis in interpretive content analysis is to summarize the data while not losing divergent views and nuance. Where context shapes meaning, context must also be fully explicated to the reader. The selection of narrative descriptions requires judgment and care to avoid bias or overemphasis on some themes or meanings.

In the three exemplar interpretive content analysis studies examined in this chapter, only Reagan's (2010) study used rough statistical estimates of theme frequency. Interpretive content analysis may or may not include descriptive statistics. Most, however, employ only narrative data analysis methods. In contrast, use of descriptive statistics as a method of data analysis and establishing the relative importance of themes is very common in basic content analysis. This is one key difference between the two approaches.

Bloom (1980) summarizes a range of data about the definition of prevention in a conceptual manner. This fits well with his research purpose and objectives. Bloom provides a narrative summary to the reader, with an emphasis on the conceptual components of prevention stated by earlier authors. In such an analytic summary, care must be taken to avoid excluding potentially disconfirming or exceptional data that do not fit the emerging definition of prevention. Researcher judgment must be applied to determine how much variety would be useful to the reader. At the same time, providing divergent data can be a helpful method of establishing validity or credibility with the reader.

Where context is crucial to establishing the meaning within coded data set, researchers must make sure that they provide readers with enough contextual data to understand its role in meaning making. Researchers should provide their readers with some examples that demonstrate how context shaped meaning and interpretation. Notably, Reagan (2010) completed her interpretive content analyses with very little analytic focus on how contexts shaped their researcher interpretations. In contrast, Barnes' (2008) participants did address their life contexts explicitly, and this focus was addressed in the data analysis. Bloom (1980) drew on the variety and contexts of application of prior definitions of prevention to identify the core elements of this concept. How context shapes meaning, and how it is shapes data analysis, is a central feature of interpretive content analysis.

How researchers understand and analyze latent content is a key issue in interpretive content analysis. Reagan (2010) chose to keep her analysis quite close to the explicit or manifest content in the student evaluation texts that were her data set. Her analysis and data reduction involved grouping coded data in ways that involved some modest researcher interpretation of shared meaning. Still, Reagan did not highlight the interpretation of latent content in her analysis. In contrast, Barnes (2008) used lengthy quotations to establish the nuance and context of her participants' statements about infant mortality in the African-American community. Several latent issues of discrimination, access to care, and quality of care emerged to provide perspective on these women's views on the complexity of infant mortality issues. Researchers undertaking interpretive content analyses may analyze and interpret latent content, but they must take care to show their readers how they make meaning of the data.

RESEARCHER SELF-REFLECTION AND REFLEXIVITY IN INTERPRETIVE CONTENT ANALYSIS

Since the researcher is the instrument of coding and other analytic decision in interpretive content analysis, self-reflection and reflexivity are important elements of the research process. Reflexivity in qualitative research addresses researcher engagement in explicit self-aware reviews of several kinds. These may range from individual self-awareness and self-reflection to intersubjective or collaborative processes to critical analyses. Finlay (2002) has identified five variants of reflexivity: (1) introspection, (2) intersubjective reflection, (3) mutual collaboration, (4) social critique, and (5) discursive deconstruction.

The purpose of self-reflection and reflexivity is to identify personal biases or views that may affect conceptual, methodological, and analytic decisions made during the project. Identifying such bias allows alterations in methods to address them or account for them in other ways. It also informs the reader of areas in which the researcher's choices may warrant careful review. As Finlay states (2002, p. 215), "the challenge for researchers using introspection is to use personal revelation not as an end in itself but as a springboard for interpretations and more general insight." That is, self-reflection is useful when it aids achievement of the overall research objectives. Such personal revelations may address intersubjective issues or more macro-level social critique.

Reagan states (2010, p. 68), "I was very aware that my role as researcher could not be separated from my personal experiences as both a long-term adult student and an experienced college teacher." These experiences may be useful toward understanding the study content and participants' views. Yet they may also serve as blinders or sources of misunderstanding or bias. In contrast to the "bracketing" techniques used in phenomenological research (Carpenter, 2007), interpretive content analysis encourages the use and review of one's own experiences and background knowledge and values. This interpretive content analysis model is more similar to Glaser and Strauss' (1967) concept of theoretical sensitivity, although it is used descriptively rather than to build theory. In the exemplar studies presented in this chapter, neither Reagan (2010) nor Barnes (2008) explicitly noted researcher self-reflection or reflexivity as components used in their studies. Instead, each researcher employed methods to enhance credibility, specifically member checks. In member checks, participants review versions of researcher-generated summarized results. The participants may affirm the researchers' summary as credible or question parts of it or the entire summary (Morse, 1994).

Most interpretive content analyses are "realist tales" (Van Maanen, 1983) in which the researcher does not engage in much formal self-reflection or reflexivity. Instead, interpretive content analyses emphasize unproblematized (more or less), objective "facts." This perspective is consistent with positivist or realist epistemologies, but not with a constructivist epistemology. Interpretive content analysis may, in part, be distinguished from qualitative content analysis based on chosen epistemologies and limited use of researcher self-reflection of reflexivity. That said, considerable additional work is needed to develop clarity regarding how choices of epistemology and techniques of self-reflection and reflexivity are applied in interpretive content analysis.

CHAPTER SUMMARY

Interpretive content analysis expands on basic content analysis by allowing more researcher exploration of latent meaning and the context of communications. This method has not been widely used in the social work research literature, but it is a valuable approach for some studies. Interpretive content analysis may be applied to existing texts as well as to newly collected primary data. It is generally predicated on either a positivist or realist epistemological base. Interpretive content analysis is most often used in descriptive research designs, but can be used in exploratory, comparative, and even predictive research designs as well.

The coding of unstructured data in interpretive content analysis employs techniques drawn from several qualitative research approaches and addresses both manifest and latent content in context. Interpretive content analyses most often take the form of summary narrative descriptions, though some studies include descriptive statistics to illustrate the relative frequencies of participants' responses. Interpretive content analyses can provide a useful evidence base for scholarship and advocacy.

Chapter 4 will examine innovations in qualitative content analysis that further extend the methods of content analysis to a wider range of research purposes. Qualitative content analyses overlap in several ways with what we call interpretive content analyses, but offer a still wider range of methods to researchers.

4

Qualitative Content Analysis

This chapter will examine qualitative content analysis. Following an introduction to qualitative content analysis and a brief history, the differences between qualitative content analysis and other qualitative research methods will be briefly addressed. Next, qualitative content analysis will be defined and two exemplar studies analyzed in detail. Further, as in Chapters 2 and 3, this chapter will examine content analysis conceptualization, practical issues, and methods using a standard outline. This structure will guide the reader in both planning a new study and reviewing completed studies. The components of qualitative content analysis include (1) research purposes, (2) epistemological issues, (3) research designs, (4) target audiences, (5) ethical issues, (6) sampling issues and methods, (7) collecting data, (8) coding methods, (9) data analysis methods and (10) the role of researcher reflection. In combination, these 10 components can help researchers appraise the overall integrity and rigor of a content analysis proposal or of a completed project.

INTRODUCTION

Mayring (2010) describes qualitative content analysis as a set of techniques for the systematic analysis of texts of many kinds, addressing not only manifest content but also the themes and core ideas found in texts as primary content. Further, as the name implies, qualitative content analysis does not employ statistical analytic methods. This definition makes qualitative content analysis similar to, yet distinct from, several other qualitative research methods.

Researchers can distinguish qualitative content analysis from other named qualitative research methods with different research purposes and methodologies. For example, discourse analysis examines naturally occurring communication events in terms of sequences, such as speaker turn-taking, propositions, or other forms of speech (Harris, 1952). Sounds, gestures, and syntax may all be foci of discourse analysis studies, as may differences among genres of discourse such as political discourse, media, education, business, and science (Harris, 1985). The focus of discourse analysis and of conversation analysis is on the elements and forms of speech, in contrast to the focus on meaning in content analysis (Gee, 2005).

Critical theory is another scholarly approach using reflective assessment and critique of social and cultural structures through the application of theory and knowledge from the social sciences and the humanities. Drawing broadly on Habermas (1968), critical theory studies use interpretation to explore the meaning of texts and symbolic expressions, including the interpretation of texts that interpret still other texts. Contemporary critical social analyses use self-reflective and reflexive knowledge to understand and explain socially structured systems of power and domination. These critical methods are hermeneutic in nature, requiring extensive interpretation that often goes beyond describing and summarizing the overt content found in texts studied. While qualitative content analyses may involve interpretations of latent content and meaning, broad critical analyses are not commonly their main research purpose. Content analyses usually maintain a more descriptive focus.

Researchers sometimes describe qualitative content analysis as sharing techniques with other forms of qualitative research. For example, Berg (2001, 2008) suggests that "open coding," the first step of coding in

Glaser and Straus's (1967) grounded theory method, may also be used in content analysis. However, the research purpose of grounded theory is to generate locally applicable concepts and theory, while content analysis focuses more on description and generally does not seek to develop theory. Further, no approach to content analysis goes on from initial "open" coding to include Glaser and Strauss' (1967) axial and discriminate coding techniques—all clear parts of grounded theory methods. It may be more useful and more rigorous to differentiate an initial step in the iterative development of grounded theory from descriptive coding of content.

What researchers vaguely label as "thematic analysis" may be most similar to contemporary qualitative content analysis. Braun and Clarke (2006, p. 4) state that thematic analysis is a "poorly demarcated and rarely acknowledged, yet widely used qualitative analytic method." This is equally so in social work publications. Indeed, there is no standard method of thematic analysis. Boyatzis' (1988) thematic analysis appears most similar to what is emerging today as qualitative content analysis. Boyatzis focuses on coding content in texts descriptively, as does qualitative content analysis. Similarly, Saldaña (2009) offers methods for coding descriptive themes that are quite similar to the processes described by Mayring (2000, 2007) and Schreier (2012). Summarizing meaning in primary or secondary data is the focus of thematic analysis. Thematic analysis may be an early, underdeveloped, variant of contemporary qualitative content analysis.

SOME HISTORICAL PERSPECTIVE

The distinction between quantitative and qualitative approaches to content analysis has long been the focus of academic discussion Kracauer (1952) argued that quantitative approaches to content analysis were often limited. He argued three key points: (1) that meaning is not always manifest; (2) that meaning is often complex, contextual, and best determined holistically; and (3) that some meaningful content may appear only once in a text, which does not necessarily mean it is not important or meaningful. For these reasons, Kracauer argued for developing qualitative approaches to content analyses. Ritsert (1972) pointed out two additional limitations to basic quantitative content analysis. He notes that the distinctive nature of individual cases may be lost in manifest content analysis and that communications that do not appear overtly in the text may be overlooked. Omissions of expected content, or the removal of content, require contextualized analyses.

Note that both Kracauer's and Ritsert's critiques address several aspects of the content analysis process. Coding becomes more complex if not all meaning is manifest or literal. Both interpretive and qualitative content analyses share this concern. Determining the validity/credibility and the reliability/trustworthiness of codes may also require different standards from those applied in basic content analysis. Further, if meaning is contextual and complex, differences in interpretation may be more common in qualitative content analysis. That is, the different backgrounds and knowledge of each coder may have a greater influence on coding. Such a perspective may be linked to a constructivist epistemology in some research endeavors. Finally, simple counts of word frequencies may not be a sufficient analytic approach. The reductionism inherent in quantification may not adequately capture certain kinds of meanings. This implies that analytic methods other than the use of descriptive or inferential statistics may be required in qualitative content analyses.

George (1959b) also argued for a "non-frequency" approach to content analysis. His work analyzing Nazi propaganda made clear that meaning was often complex, contextual, and "latent." In addition, George, found that pivotal information might be present only once in a number of texts. George's research supports Kracauer's (1952) claim that key evidence may appear only once, or rarely, in collected data. These researchers also point out that such pivotal information might not be valued appropriately by summary statistical analytic methods. Varied research purposes and objectives clearly suggest that a range of content analysis methodologies might be useful.

If a qualitative approach to content analysis is needed, what would such an approach need to include? To begin, the role of content in qualitative research generally must be examined.

The General Role of "Content" in Qualitative Research

It is fair to argue that virtually all qualitative research addresses the *content* of texts, whether the "texts" are books, images, physical artifacts, audio files, video files, or other media. Qualitative research methods may describe the content found in texts, or they may summarize the key themes found in texts, or examine the process or form of the delivery of content, or seek to develop a conceptualization of the content. Sandeloswki (2000) states that the variety of qualitative research methods makes renewed attention to qualitative description useful and necessary. Yet how to distinguish qualitative content analysis from the wider range of alternative qualitative methods may prove challenging. Indeed, some named qualitative research methods appear to be very similar to qualitative content analysis. Boyatzis' (1998) thematic analysis and Hill's (2011) consensual qualitative analysis both appear very similar to the core methods identified by other authors as qualitative content analysis.

As with many models of qualitative research, there are variations evident within a particular, named research method. Schreier (2014b) listed 11 "named" variants of qualitative content analysis that she found in the international interdisciplinary literature. These ranged from content-structuring analyses, to analysis of images, to evaluative content analyses, to directed analysis and summative content analysis. Qualitative content analysis has several developers and advocates, each with somewhat different emphases and research purposes. All address the content of research data sets to some extent. So just what defines qualitative content analysis?

WHAT IS QUALITATIVE CONTENT ANALYSIS?

Mayring (2010), a German psychologist who appears to have first used the term in 1983, states that *qualitative content analysis* is a set of techniques for the systematic analysis of texts of many kinds addressing not only manifest content but also the themes and core ideas found in texts as primary content. Contextual information and latent content are included in qualitative content analysis. Analysis of the formal aspects of the content may also be included. "Formal aspects" here means how narratives are formatted and delivered; it includes form and processes as well as overt content. According to Mayring (2000, para 5), "qualitative content analysis defines itself . . . as an approach of empirical, methodological controlled analysis of texts within their context of communication, following content analytical rules and step by step models, without rash quantification." The model is intended to build on the strengths of other content analysis models while respecting context and latent communication. Validity and reliability are emphasized in qualitative content analysis (Mayring, 2000; Schreier, 2012), rather than credibility and trustworthiness, which reflect a more constructivist epistemology. Statistics are rarely, if ever, used in data analysis. Further, the model allows for exploring the complexity of communications in ways that may not be possible through quantitative analyses.

Mayring (2000) cites a number of studies using qualitative content analysis. For example, Vicini (1993) conducted open-ended interviews with educational advisors to identify inductively their theories of advising. Bauer, Qualmann, Stadtmüller, and Bauer (1998) examined the biographies of people with Alzheimer's disease and contrasted their narratives with those of people who had cardiovascular problems. The researchers found more overprotective social networks among the people with Alzheimer's disease. Note that data sets based on newly generated interviews are common in qualitative content analysis (as they are in interpretive content analysis). Qualitative content analysis may be used to explore new topics, describe complex phenomena in open systems, compare and contrast group differences, and develop and test theories.

Sandelowski (2000, p. 338) draws on English-language authors to advocate for qualitative content analysis as the "strategy of choice in qualitative descriptive studies." Drawing on the work of Altheide (1987) and Morgan (1993), she describes qualitative content analysis as a form of analysis for verbal and visual data oriented toward summarizing the informational content of the data set. Sandelowski emphasizes that, in contrast to basic content analysis, researchers typically inductively generate codes from the data rather than apply deductively generated codes derived from prior theory and research. This allows data collection and data analysis to be undertaken simultaneously and flexibly in order to capture context and nuance.

However, in contrast to basic and interpretive approaches to content analysis, a description of patterns or regularities found in the data is the goal of qualitative content analysis (Crabtree & Miller, 1999; Tesch, 1990). Sandelowski (2000, p. 338) states that "qualitative content analysis moves farther into the domain of interpretation than quantitative [basic] content analysis in that there is an effort to understand not only the manifest (e.g., frequencies and means) but also the latent content of data." Yet she also notes that qualitative content analysis is the least interpretive of all forms of qualitative research "in that there is no mandate to re-present the data in any other terms but their own" (p. 338). This, in Sandelowski's view, makes qualitative content analysis the ideal approach to descriptive qualitative research. Narrative summaries of ideas and themes are common in reports of such research. Indeed, many qualitative studies in the social work literature appear to fit this model of descriptive qualitative research in which the researchers summarize or catalogue the newly collected or existing collected data.

Qualitative content analysis may be a little known and poorly understood but widely used form of social work research. Schreier (2014b) notes that there are "inconsistent explanations as to what actually constitutes the method of qualitative content analysis." Krippendorff (2013), for example, includes discourse or conversation analysis among qualitative content analysis techniques. In contrast to Sandelowski's view, Schreier (2012) argues that researchers may use inductively created or deductive generated approaches to coding or a mix of both. She emphasizes the central importance of coding and validity to qualitative content analysis. Like Sandelowski, Schreier (2014b) emphasizes the descriptive focus of qualitative content analysis as a process for the categorization of selected text meanings. To Schreier (2014b, para 4), "both the creation and the application of the category system is done interpretively and allows for the inclusion of latent content. . . . The approach is systematic, rule governed, and shaped by criteria of validity and reliability." Researchers seek intersubjective and consensual understanding of texts, though not necessarily through the use of quantitative inter-rater coefficients.

Schreier (2014b) states that qualitative content analysis seeks to expand on the textual data on which it is based. In contrast to the data reduction purpose of basic content analysis, qualitative content analyses may actually expand on or enlarge the original data. This is one key difference between qualitative content analysis and the basic and interpretive approaches.

Overall, qualitative content analysis refers to a systematic method for searching out and describing meanings within texts of many kinds (Kohlbacher, 2005; Morgan, 1993). Both manifest and latent content are examined, as are meanings in context. As we shall see, authors may portray coding in qualitative content analysis as theory based and deductive, or as data grounded and inductive, or as a mix of both approaches. The focus of qualitative content analysis is often on identifying categories or themes that both summarize the content found in the full data set and highlight key content. To achieve this goal, the meaning of content may be interrogated and expanded.

Oddly, researchers do not explicitly address issues of epistemology in the qualitative content analysis literature. Sandelowski (2000) appears to represent a positivist or realist epistemology emphasizing little interpretation, while Mayring (2000), Morgan (1993), and Schreier (2012, 2014b) appear to represent a constructivist epistemological stance emphasizing multiple perspectives and the importance of researcher interpretation. The lack of attention to the shaping role of epistemologies is an area in need of further development in qualitative content analysis.

Examples of Qualitative Content Analysis in the Social Work Literature

The *Social Work Abstracts* database showed 30 qualitative content analyses as of March 2015. Researchers will find many more qualitative content analyses in the larger databases of other professions.

Johnston-Goodstar, Richards-Schuster, and Sethi (2014) examined the online mission statements and written descriptions of youth media programs. Their research questions included, "How do youth media practitioners articulate their 'work'?" and "What frameworks do they use?" While the authors note the need for further development of ethical standards for online research, they do not specifically address obtaining institutional review board approval. This was likely due to their use of public online documents that do not appear to contain more than everyday risks. The researchers analyzed and reviewed materials from 49 youth media programs, inductively identifying main categories such as "youth media as a tool for empowerment," and "youth media as a tool for social action" (p. 4). Subcategories within the empowerment main category included "building leadership skills," "promoting leadership and self-confidence," and "telling their own stories" (p. 4). The authors cite Braun and Clarke (2013) as their methodological source in applying key qualitative content analysis methods to publicly available online data. (Braun and Clarke's textbook specifically addresses content analysis on only one introductory page.)

In another example, Chan et al. (2012) collected narratives about contemporary filial piety and end-of-life care from 15 Hong Kong Chinese caregivers. The sample included stage IV terminal cancer patients at one hospital. With prior university institutional review board approval, the researchers solicited caregivers through purposive sampling. The researchers used what they called a modified grounded theory approach to coding. Yet they also stated that they sought to generate descriptive themes within the participants' narratives rather than a conceptual model or mid-level theory. (As noted earlier, open coding in grounded theory is the first of three iterative stages of coding. It is also focused on developing concepts rather than simply summarizing or describing views and events—the descriptive focus of qualitative content analysis. The technique of open coding is applied here to a different research purpose than that of grounded theory research.) Chan et al. used Neimeyer's (2001; Neimeyer & Sands, 2011) methods of "meaning reconstruction" for their analysis.

Chan et al.'s team of researchers coded five themes or main categories, including "reciprocal relationships and mutual support." The themes described contemporary views of filial piety that they contrasted with more traditional cultural views. For example, Chinese parents traditionally have expected their children to conform to their wishes without resistance. Contemporary caregivers, however, often have to look after their parents while maintaining work commitments and providing care for their own children. This might involve negotiations requiring some flexibility of both the parent and caregiver. The researchers used the category "reciprocal relationships" to describe the more flexible nature of these interactions, in contrast to traditional expectations of deference to the parent's wishes. Participants might not have used the specific terminology of the category label; therefore, an interpretive analysis was required. The researchers captured the meaning of the participants' narratives in the codes, though the specific content of their stories differed. No statistics were used by Chan and colleagues.

Qualitative content analysis can be a useful research method for the study of diverse populations. It may be undertaken in a culturally competent manner to overcome a number of limitations present in other research methods (Lee & Zaharlick, 2013).

RESEARCH PURPOSES OF QUALITATIVE CONTENT ANALYSIS

As noted previously in the definitions of qualitative content analysis, many authors view it as an optimal method for describing meaning in communications (Mayring, 2000, 2010; Morgan, 1993; Sandelowski, 2000; Schreier, 2012). One aspect of such description is frequently to categorize the manifest and/or latent and contextualized content into a narrative summary. Such categorization may be topical, formal, or hierarchical. Qualitative content analysts generally view their approach as more focused on description than on conceptual development; yet any form of categorization will arguably involve some degree of abstraction. Categorization is also a form of data reduction or summarizing that may be useful in analyses of large data sets or simply to clarify the key points within texts. Schreier (2014b) also suggests that qualitative content analysis may expand on the original data and actually enlarge it.

Krippendorff (2013) has identified three kinds of research designs to which content analysis may be applied: (1) exploratory/descriptive, in which knowledge of content and contexts is described or more clearly defined; (2) explanatory tests of hypotheses that examine the merit and utility of specified analytical constructs; and (3) explanatory tests of discriminant function that affirm or negate the explanatory power and utility of specified constructs. Qualitative content analysis can be applied to both the exploratory/descriptive purposes Krippendorff addresses and qualitatively testing the merits of specific analytic constructs. Qualitative content analysis could also serve as a starting point for later quantification and explanatory research using discriminate function or path analysis techniques. Neimeyer (2001) also views qualitative content analysis as a potential first step toward a later quantities analysis. There are, however, no clear examples of such uses in the social work literature to date.

EPISTEMOLOGICAL FOUNDATIONS OF QUALITATIVE CONTENT ANALYSIS

All research of merit begins with a good research question (Drisko, 2013b). Criteria for identifying a good research question include its importance, fruitfulness, timeliness, interest to a specific audience, and utility to problem-solving. Assuming a worthy research question is posed, *how* the question will be examined is the next step. A key step is to select an epistemology to guide the research project. Epistemological choices influence in important ways several later decisions about research methods and the interpretation of research results.

Surprisingly, the literature on qualitative content analysis does not explicitly address the role of epistemology. Hints about the role of epistemology are found throughout this literature, but little direct discussion is evident. For example, Schreier (2012) lists and contrasts features that distinguish quantitative and qualitative research. She includes attention to naturalistic studies (rather than those involving manipulation), the importance of context, inferences based on context, author and recipient of communication, and elaboration rather than the reduction of data. Yet many American scholars would view the importance of these elements as being due to non- or post-positivist or constructivist ways of knowing. Many core issues raised in the qualitative content analysis literature seem to center on the role of epistemology in research.

Some scholars argue that *all* qualitative research is constructivist in epistemology (Denzin & Lincoln, 2005). Denzin and Lincoln base their position on a vision of qualitative research as situated in specific contexts and the co-creation of results by participants and researchers. Constructivist research is defined by an epistemological stance: that social knowledge is the active product of human "knowers," that knowledge is situated and relative, that it varies across people and their social groups, and that it is context-dependent (Drisko, 2013a). Experiences in the natural and the social world are "constructed" using the interpretive categories of one's reference group. There are multiple realities based on peoples' varied interpretative constructs and categories (Drisko, 2013a). Constructivists do not deny the reality of the external world; rather, they understand that knowledge of the world is related to the ways in which we actively organize our experiences of it (von Glaserfeld, 1984). In many respects, qualitative content analysis presumes that contextualized and latent communications may not be immediately evident to all readers. Differences in interpretation are understood as inevitable; what is important for research is to make explicit how and why interpretations were made. How to make useful and meaningful interpretations of latent and contextualized data is central to qualitative content analysis.

Explicitly adopting a constructivist epistemology for qualitative content analysis has consequences for how the method is conceptualized and undertaken (Drisko, 2013b). The use of positivist, quantitative terminology, including the terms *validity* and *reliability*, is problematic from a constructivist epistemology. Many qualitative researchers acknowledge multiple ways of knowing and multiple perspectives on a single event or idea. *Credibility* and *trustworthiness* are the terms used in place of *validity*, reflecting multiple standpoints and meanings (Drisko, 1997; 2013a). The concepts of credibility and trustworthiness do not assume simple correspondence between facts or experiences and the ways people describe or make meaning of these facts or experiences. Further, qualitative research generally seeks to be meaningful in context rather than universally applicable. Confirmability and completeness or saturation also matter in qualitative research. Member checks—collaborative reviews of data summaries and analyses with research participants—is a technique used to ensure that reports reflect the voices and views of others. Of course, member checks may not be possible with authors of some texts, but they are frequently possible with research participants who offer new data for content analysis. Confirmability, accuracy, and trustworthiness replace statistical approaches to reliability in studies using a constructivist epistemology (Drisko, 1997; 2013b). Generalizability is inherently limited to specific people in a specific era and context. Yet virtually none of these concepts or issues are explored currently in the English-language or German qualitative content analysis literature.

Qualitative content analysis, across its several variants, appears to draw on a constructivist epistemology. Such an epistemology would fit well with the interpretive emphasis of this approach. More direct exploration of how epistemology influences qualitative content analysis and its research methods would be very useful and timely. Such exploration may also be useful in clarifying the differences between interpretive and qualitative content analysis and among the variants of qualitative content analysis.

RESEARCH DESIGNS IN QUALITATIVE CONTENT ANALYSIS

Most scholars view qualitative content analysis as descriptive in focus and design (Mayring, 2010; Sandelowski, 2000; Sandelowski & Barroso,

2003; Schreier, 2012). While the method clearly describes key meanings within a data set, it may also be useful as an exploratory research design used to identify new ways of looking at events and communications (Sandelowski & Barroso, 2003). That is, qualitative content analyses of new phenomena or diverse populations or novel settings may simultaneously *explore* new intellectual territory as it *describes* what was found. For example, the Chan et al. (2012) study detailed earlier appears to be both exploratory and descriptive in design simultaneously. Qualitative content analyses may be exploratory in design, descriptive, or both at once.

Schreier (2014b) points out that qualitative content analysis may be used for *evaluation, comparative designs*, and even in *explanatory* research designs. For example, Kuckartz (2012) applied qualitative content analysis using rank-ordered categories in order to evaluate individual and group differences. Researchers could use such comparative methods to test hypothesized differences among groups. For example, Bauer et al. (1998) compared the biographies of persons with Alzheimer's disease to those of persons with cardiovascular problems. Given a set of guiding hypotheses that prior research suggests differentiate these two populations, a qualitative content analysis could be one way to test that such group differences are empirically grounded.

Mayring (2010) further suggests that qualitative content analysis may be used to more fully explicate the meaning of a text. In Mayring's model, aspects of text and context are examined jointly to show more fully how meaning is shaped. This allows for an explanation of the meaning(s) found in a text, as well as for a description of how such meanings are conveyed. Schreier (2014b) points out that such an explicative use of qualitative content analysis actually expands and enlarges on the original material. This is a very different research purpose than the more typical data-reductive aspect of most content analyses.

Data Reduction in Qualitative Content Analysis

Schreier (2014b) states that qualitative content analyses may involve data reduction through the analytic use of descriptive categories or themes. The goal in such studies is to identify and highlight the most relevant and meaningful passages of text. Researchers may also illustrate the kinds of variation found within specific categories or themes.

Qualitative content analysis may summarize larger data sets and generates typologies of content related to the researcher's purposes and questions.

Schreier (2014b) also notes that qualitative content analyses may interrogate, expand on, and enlarge the data in order to explicate its meaning and its nuance. While reports of qualitative content analysis may provide a reductive summary of that data under study, the process of generating this summary may be expansive rather than reductive. Such an expansion of the data during analysis is a key feature of qualitative content analysis.

TARGET AUDIENCES FOR QUALITATIVE CONTENT ANALYSIS

There are very few qualitative content analyses in the social work literature. Twenty-eight articles and five dissertations between 1979 and 2014 were listed in the *Social Work Abstracts* database as of March 2015. These studies explore diverse topics, including youth media, pro-anorexia perspectives, financial planning, social policy, and professional education. It appears that most of these studies target other academics and practitioners as their key audiences.

At the same time, most qualitative content analysis reports include advocacy for particular points of view or for specific practice or policy efforts. Advocacy efforts based on qualitative content analysis routinely involve abductive inferences. That is, authors use the qualitative content analysis findings as a jumping-off point for wider advocacy claims that extend somewhat beyond the data. For example, Johnston-Goodstar, Richards-Schuster, and Sethi (2014, abstract) completed a qualitative content analysis on youth media. They also applied a critical media literacy framework "to analyze the practice of these youth media groups and apply those findings to social work practice, education, and research." The authors then used the findings of the qualitative content analysis abductively as an evidence base for making related advocacy claims. These advocacy efforts may extend abductively beyond the actual data, showing how the data can inform applied improvements in practice and policy. Such abductive arguments are also common in basic and interpretive content analysis. The rigor of the qualitative content analysis either can serve to strengthen the argument for such advocacy or may help point out its limitations.

ETHICAL ISSUES IN QUALITATIVE CONTENT ANALYSIS

Given prior harms to human research participants done by well-intended researchers, it is always wise and ethically sound to seek a formal institutional review before undertaking any research involving people. Ethics review regulations in the United States allow institutional review boards to determine that studies are exempt from review where risks are no greater than everyday hazards, to allow an expedited review where risks are slight, or to require a full review where risks are potentially more serious. Researchers doing any form of content analysis should seek review of their projects by an authorized ethics review board.

Readers will find a more complete discussion of ethical issues pertinent to both basic and interpretive content analysis in Chapter 2. A summary of ethical concerns specific to interpretive content analysis is offered here.

Qualitative content analyses may employ either existing data sets or newly collected data. Where existing data are used and draw from materials in the public domain, review by an institutional ethics panel may not be required. Altheide and Schneider (2013) minimally address the place of ethics and informed consent in their book, *Qualitative Media Analysis*. This may be because they view the use of publicly available media as open for research use. However, many studies in the English- and German-language literature involve the collection of new data from human research participants via interviews. Vicini's (1993) interview-based analysis of theories of educational advising is an example of the use of newly collected data in qualitative content analysis. Studies drawing on newly collected data from human research participants will always require institutional ethics review. It appears that qualitative content analyses are more likely to involve the collection of new data than are basic or interpretive content analyses, though *all* approaches to content analysis may use such data.

As noted in Chapter 2, use of certain electronic data sets, such as social media postings, may constitute a gray area for ethics review and informed consent. People who post to such sites may not view their information as public, though this may be a naive viewpoint. Where such data are used in content analysis, institutional review is indicated to avoid ethical missteps.

To date, there appears to be very little discussion of ethical issues in the qualitative content analysis literature. Ethical issues are not mentioned in Schreier's (2012) text on qualitative content analysis practice or in its index. This omission persists despite the publication of many articles identified as qualitative content analysis that use newly collected data. Indeed, the qualitative content analysis literature emphasizes the use of newly collected data sets (see, for example, the illustrative studies mentioned by Mayring 2000, 2010; and by Schreier 2012, 2014b). Researchers must undertake further conceptualization to clarify the ethical issues posed by qualitative content analyses.

Prior institutional review of all research involving the collection of new data from human research participants should always be undertaken. Such projects should all have prior ethics review board approval. Notice of this approval, and efforts to protect human research participants, should be briefly reported in all publications using the data set.

SAMPLING IN QUALITATIVE CONTENT ANALYSIS

Scholars minimally address the topic of sampling in the current qualitative content analysis literature. Neither Schreier (2012) nor Mayring (2000) specifically addresses sampling as a topic. Sandelowski (2000) and Zhang and Wildemuth (2009) argue briefly for the use of purposive sampling in qualitative content analysis. Only Elo et al. (2014) have addressed sample size and representativeness in terms of how such decisions influence the transferability and trustworthiness of a qualitative content analysis. Yet the nature of the sample may strongly affect the credibility and applicability of a qualitative content analysis.

The authors of most social work texts typically conceptualize qualitative research sampling as a single, fixed step occurring before data collection (Drisko, 2003). This conceptualization is incomplete and often misleading: Qualitative sampling is better understood as an ongoing iterative process co-occurring with data collection and data analysis (Drisko, 2003; LeCompte & Preissle, 1993). Such iterative sampling helps in obtaining an adequate and thorough sample for descriptive studies of groups or other open systems that do not have fixed and invariant boundaries. Iterative sampling is also helpful in providing a complete basis for theory development. Further, terminology related to qualitative research sampling is used inconsistently in the research literature, reducing clarity for readers and learners alike (Drisko, 2003).

Sampling and the Quality of the Data Set

Some standards for qualitative sampling can be identified in the literature. First, samples for qualitative research must be appropriate to the research question, whether they are fixed prior to data collection or iterative (LeCompte & Preissle, 1993; Maxwell, 1996; Miles & Huberman, 1984). Second, samples must be "information rich" (LeCompte & Preissle, 1993; Patton, 1990, p. 169). That is, samples must be adequate to the exploration of the research question (Patton, 1990). Fortune and Reid (1999) note that research samples may fail to provide requisite information. For example, a study of couples' interactions may include only one partner rather than both. Such a sample is neither appropriate nor adequate.

Another hazard of sample selection prior to data collection is that the obtained sample may not provide information that is adequate for thorough exploration of the research question. A flexible, iterative approach to sampling allows different types of sampling efforts to ensure adequate information. A key strength of the iterative sampling process is the opportunity to expand or otherwise alter the sample to provide adequate information. A third standard for qualitative research samples is that samples must be thorough in the sense that they include potentially disconfirming or elaborating evidence (LeCompte & Preissle, 1993). This idea may be implicit in the second standard but merits explicit statement. The obligation to seek and examine potentially disconfirming evidence is central to rigorous research (Drisko, 1997, 2013b). Yet another strength of iterative sampling is that there is both the expectation and opportunity to seek cases that can challenge or enhance the researcher's initial understanding of the research question.

Elo et al. (2014, p. 4) state that "a disadvantage of purposive sampling is that it can be difficult for the reader to judge the trustworthiness of sampling if full details are not provided." Solid, transparent, descriptions of sampling plans are needed to ensure rigor in qualitative content analysis. Further, readers often have to determine if the results of a particular sample are transferable to people and settings of their interest. Small purposive samples often point to potentially important and useful results in an exploratory manner, but critical thinking and additional research are often needed to ensure transferability of results to other settings and populations. As in most qualitative research, the yield of qualitative content analysis generally suggests new ways of thinking or doing practice. It raises reader's awareness and theoretical sensitivity but does not claim to demonstrate transferability. The applicability of qualitative content analysis results to new setting must be tested in the new settings to demonstrate their usefulness.

It is worth noting that the generalizability of most quantitative studies, including quantitative content analyses, is often similarly limited. Generalizing from probability samples is limited to the population from which the probability sample was originally drawn. If this is a set of documents, or even a listing of social workers from a single state, the generalizability of results only extends to the original population of texts or to the social workers within the single state. Care must always be taken in applying the results of research to populations and settings beyond that used in the original study.

Qualitative Sampling Terminology

Qualitative research may employ probability sampling methods if they adequately address the research question and purposes. (Probability sampling is examined in depth in Chapter 2 of this book.) However, most qualitative studies and qualitative content analyses employ non-probability or purposive samples. There are several forms of purposive sampling.

Purposive sampling is employed to raise awareness, provide new perspectives, or provide descriptions of events, beliefs, and actions. That is, a profile of some action, attitude, event, or belief is developed from the data provided by several informants or texts. The data set seeks to describe unknown information or perspectives, explicate new meanings, and create new awareness and sensitivity in the reader. This informative, or sensitizing, use of purposive sample selection is relatively free of risk as long as no claim of transferability or generalization to a larger group with different characteristics is implied (Patton, 1980). It may, however, be overreaching to claim that purposive sample selection alone can provide an accurate portrait of the group from which it is drawn. Any such claim of transferability is made more difficult when the group is an open system lacking clear and fixed boundaries. Transferability is analytic and inductive, not numeric or probabilistic (Patton, 1990).

Many other named techniques of sampling are also purposive in nature. Patton's (1980, 1990) *"typical case"* sample selection targets average cases. Such cases may be very appropriate in descriptive qualitative research and in qualitative content analysis. One significant challenge to such typical case selection is that it requires, prior to case selection, that "certain information must be known about the variation among cases" (Patton, 1980, p. 100). Such information is often unknown to the researcher. This is especially so when the researcher is studying an open system or group with no obvious or fixed boundaries, or when the researcher has no prior theory on which to draw. For example, the "typical user" of a mental health clinic may not be determined without prior information or considerable observation and interviewing. Nomination of typical cases by group members may be helpful but is not necessarily accurate or complete. The clinic's administration may be able to profile typical cases on a quantitative basis, but this does not guarantee that these people will be able to provide useful and information-rich data.

Critical case sampling focuses on theoretically determined key informants (Patton, 1990). Critical cases are selected to provide particularly valuable perspectives and insights. They may be pivotal cases, "bellwether" cases, or cases that provide additional theoretical and perspectival richness in contrast to typical cases. *Intensity sampling* has a similar logic (Patton, 1990). Cases are selected that are theoretically determined to offer depth and/or breadth on a given event, belief, or other topic of interest. Researchers purposefully select such cases over others for their potential to yield valuable information and to clarify the impact of contexts. In both methods, transferability or generalization is not typically sought nor expected; information richness on a selected topic is the key concern.

Unique, unusual, or *extreme case sampling* methods are techniques that are also purposive (Patton, 1990). Via nomination, or using observation, such unusual or extreme cases are identified and included in the sample. Extreme cases offer perspectives that are often unheard or undervalued. They can also supplement information gained more readily from typical cases in an iterative sampling process. Identifying extreme cases also requires some prior knowledge or, alternately, a concurrent appraisal of typical cases from which to distinguish the extremes (Patton, 1990). Unique or extreme cases can also provide perspectives that elaborate or enhance one's understanding of typical cases (Znaniecki, 1934). However, transferability is abstract and analytic, based on the apparent relevance or utility of the new awareness in other situations, rather than on any numerical measure of representativeness (Patton, 1980; Robinson, 1951; Znaniecki, 1934). "Logical generalization can often be made on the weight of evidence" (Patton, 1980, p. 103; see also Znaniecki, 1934).

Maximum variation sampling has a similar purpose but requires initial efforts to identify and include multiple perspectives on dimensions of interest to the researcher (Guba & Lincoln, 1989; Patton, 1980). Used descriptively in conjunction with typical case sampling, the two sampling techniques together can profile both typical cases and the range of variation around the typical cases. The completeness of the obtained sample remains uncertain, however, and transferability is analytic rather than quantitative and probabilistic. Combined typical case and maximum variation sampling would be a strong plan for many qualitative content analysis studies.

Iterative Sampling

Many prominent qualitative researchers argue that an iterative or cyclical approach to sampling yields optimal samples (Glaser & Strauss, 1967; LeCompte & Preissle, 1993; Patton, 1980). Iterative sampling is a process through which researchers review and revise their initial sampling plan based on the results of preliminary data collection and data analysis. Newly discovered information is then used to guide future sampling decisions. A cycle of sampling, data collection, and data analysis is employed to identify gaps and omissions in the sampling plan. The cycle also yields data that are thorough to the topic under study and therefore most useful for guiding data analysis and research reports. Researchers must be self-aware and reflective to avoid obtaining a biased sample or one that does not allow for variation in meanings or viewpoints as best as this can be established. The central concept is that what emerges from data analysis will shape subsequent sampling decisions. The iterative cycle continues until researchers reach *saturation*, the point at which no new information or new themes result from additional data collection and analysis.

When researchers use qualitative content analysis in an exploratory manner, small samples without an iterative sampling process can yield innovative and informative results. When researchers use qualitative content analysis in descriptive research designs, however, an iterative sampling plan should yield more complete and more nuanced results.

DATA COLLECTION IN QUALITATIVE CONTENT ANALYSIS

Elo et al. (2014) state that data collection in contemporary qualitative content analysis is most often based on newly gathered verbal data such as interview transcripts. Indeed, the studies cited by Schreier (2012) draw predominantly on interviews or on first-person narratives. One challenge in collecting such descriptive data is to maintain a focus on relevant content while preventing interviewer-generated bias or interviewer emphasis on a single viewpoint or perspective.

Open-ended questions allowing for a wide range of responses are optimal. Researchers also use semi-structured interviews effectively, though they must take care not to privilege one perspective over others. This may be a hazard where previous work points to a predominant or favored viewpoint or meaning. Researchers must be careful that deductively generated questions or emphases do not exclude efforts to seek out other potential points of view and meanings. It is recommended that questions be developed with input from knowledgeable individuals and pilot testing with an emphasis on ensuring that participants are free to respond with a variety of viewpoints (Pyett, 2003).

The self-awareness and reflective skill of the researcher is vital in planning and undertaking data collection. The clarity of the questions asked or used to select texts is of primary importance to obtaining optimally diverse and credible data. In addition, ongoing review of the collected data, in collaboration with colleagues serving as peer reviewers, can help limit bias or manipulation of participants. Commentary on research questions and methods is also a valuable source of revision to data collection techniques and strategies.

While most qualitative content analyses employ single-interview or single-narrative data, multiple interviews and repeated narratives may help ensure that any particular viewpoint or meaning is credible and reflects the participant's views fully. Padgett (1998) argues for prolonged exposure as a technique for collecting the best possible data. This recommendation may also be applicable to data collection in qualitative content analysis.

CODING IN QUALITATIVE CONTENT ANALYSIS

The first step in coding qualitative data is to become very familiar with the data set. Some scholars call this step "immersion" in the data (Miles & Huberman, 1984). Such immersion in the data set provides a sense of the study as a whole and of its component parts. It helps build awareness to context and nuance, which is important in qualitative content analysis. The goal is for the researcher to become informed about the content in context, to begin to notice key content and omissions of what might be expected content or perspectives, and to begin to identify connections within the data and preliminary categories. The purpose of coding is to develop new knowledge and to address fully the research question that frames the study. Rigorous coding requires wide-ranging, in-depth knowledge of the data set.

Schreier (2012) points to coding as a defining feature of qualitative content analysis. Researchers use coding to identify and describe key meanings within texts of many kinds. Coding is also used to reduce and summarize those meanings that are most relevant to answering the research question. In contrast to some other qualitative approaches to coding, Schreier (2012) views coding in qualitative content analysis as solely descriptive; it is not intended to begin a conceptual analysis of the content. Yet one might argue that coding, when not used merely to label segments of the data set (as is done in eidetic phenomenology) *always* involves some conceptualization. Yet Schreier emphasizes only its descriptive function. She suggests that this is one important way in which qualitative content analysis is distinguished from other qualitative research methods. Sandelowski (2000) similarly emphasizes the central role of descriptive coding in qualitative content analysis.

Given that qualitative data sets may involve literally hundreds of pages of text or other data, the first step is to identify the main categories. Main categories are also called *themes* or *dimensions* in the qualitative content literature. The term *themes* is often found in the American qualitative research literature, though its definition is broad and often imprecise (Braun & Clarke, 2013). The term *dimensions* may also be confusing to some readers familiar with other qualitative research methods, such as grounded theory, in which a dimension refers specifically to a rank-ordered concept (Glaser & Strauss, 1967). In qualitative content analysis, main categories are most often nominal-level categories that are mutually exclusive and exhaustive to the focal content (Schreier, 2012).

Once the researcher identifies main categories, subcategories are specified to elaborate on the detailed content. The subcategories serve to structure the description within each category while also providing more detail and nuance. Subcategories may also be viewed as nominal-, ordinal-, or interval-level measures (Mayring, 2010; Schreier, 2104b).

All coding requires that the researcher make ongoing determinations of what is relevant and revealing content versus that which is irrelevant (Schreier, 2012). As Krippendorff (1980, p. 76) states, "how categories are defined . . . is an art." The process of creating a coding frame, or list of codes relevant to a specific project, may be undertaken inductively, deductively, or using both approaches.

Inductive and Deductive Approaches to Coding in Qualitative Content Analysis

Several authors argue that qualitative content analysis is, in part, defined by the use of inductive approaches to coding (Mayring, 2000; Schreier, 2012). They contrast the use of "emergent" coding derived from the data as a central feature of qualitative research, in contrast to the deductive approach used in most quantitative research. Qualitative content analysts use inductive coding to create data-grounded categories and to ensure that the views and voices of research participants are given priority over the ideas and theories of the researchers. Used in exploratory and descriptive research designs, inductive coding can help keep the development of coding categories close to and grounded in the original data.

That said, a variety of coding approaches are found in the published qualitative content analysis literature. Mayring (2000) has described both inductive and deductive processes for developing coding categories. Schreier (2014b) has identified a range of qualitative content analysis models that use each process or both in combination.

Inductive Coding Development and Application

In inductive coding, researchers first formulate a working definition of a category drawing on the textual material that best captures the meaning of the content found in the original data. Initial use of "open coding" following Glaser and Strauss' (1967; also Strauss and Corbin, 1998) technique is often suggested. However, open coding in qualitative content analysis is substantive rather than focused on conceptual development. Researchers identify relevant categories and label them descriptively. Coding should initially be over-inclusive as the researcher learns and refines the meaning of the texts. Each coding category should be relevant, close to the original content, and modifiable.

One technique is to use in vivo codes (Glaser & Strauss, 1967; Strauss & Corbin, 1998), which use a word or a short phrase from the original content to literally reflect the essence of the content's meaning. Note, however, that in vivo coding may assume that the manifest content of the data is all that is needed to convey its meaning successfully. This appears a bit ironic in qualitative content analysis, a method in which latent content and its interpretation are highly emphasized. Regardless of how the researcher does initial sampling, the initial coding list will be iteratively refined as sampling, data collection, and data analysis proceed across multiple texts or participants.

Several publications self-described as qualitative content analysis refer to the use of Glaser and Strauss' (1967) grounded theory as their method of coding. It is important to understand that grounded theory research seeks to develop mid-level theory of practice or meaning making in a particular situation or setting. The goal of grounded theory is to develop concepts and ultimately a working theory that captures the views and actions of the research participants. Grounded theory is not a descriptive research method but a conceptual method, as should be evident from the name of the method. In contrast, qualitative content analysis is most often used descriptively rather than to develop concepts and theory. The yield of qualitative content analysis is most often descriptive categories and themes; conceptualization and theory are not often part of the method. In turn, the aim of coding in qualitative content analysis is not to generate concepts and theory, but instead to describe the meanings and actions of research participants and texts. Researchers must correctly understand and represent the purposes and goals of these two different research methods.

Category Development

Mayring (2000) states that inductive category development begins with defining central categories and clarifying the level of abstraction among them. As codes are developed, the next step is to determine which codes are more overarching and which are subsidiary to these central codes. A hierarchy of codes is created, with central codes as the key categories and many subsidiary codes elaborating the content in greater detail across several dimensions. Mayring (2000, para 11, Figure 1) states that after 10% to 50% of the texts are coded a "formative" reliability check of the coding frame should be undertaken and revisions made as needed. Revisions will include discarding rarely used codes (so long as they are not central to addressing the research question) and reviewing the coding hierarchy. Using the revised coding frame, the coding process then continues to completion. When coding of all texts is completed, another "summative" reliability check of the coding frame is completed (Mayring, 2000, Figure 1).

According to Mayring (2000), both the formative and summative reliability checks may lead to iterative revisions of the research question or changes in the coding categories. After the coding frame is finalized, interpretation of these inductively generated results is undertaken. While Mayring (2000) does not directly discuss the validity of the inductive coding frame, researchers should also examine how the coded material fits with and elaborates on the entire data set. Since coding may be contextual and may draw on latent content, one key issue is to create a transparent "map" of how the codes were created that is credible and clear to the reader. In studies using a constructivist epistemology, readers will be the final arbiters of the credibility and persuasiveness of the researcher's coding frame and interpretation of the data. Sufficient raw data must be provided to the reader to question and interrogate the researcher's coding work (Drisko, 2013a, 2013b).

Deductive Coding Application

Some models of qualitative content analysis begin with an orienting theory or evaluation question that allows the deductive development of at least some of the codes used in the study. In deductive coding, prior empirical research and theory are employed to derive some categories. Mayring (2000) claims that the processes for developing deductive categories are poorly developed in the qualitative content analysis literature. Mayring (2000, para 14, Figure 2) suggests that deductive category development begins with the identification of "main and subcategories from the existing literature." From this material, the researchers formulate coding definitions and/or rules. After coding part of the data set with the deductively generated categories, researchers can undertake a formative reliability check. In this formative check, examples of coded content are compared to the deductive coding frame to ensure reliability. The full data set is then coded. After coding is completed, the researchers complete a summative reliability check to again ensure reliability and the consistent application of coding rules.

While Mayring (2000) does not directly discuss the validity of the deductively generated coding frame, researchers should also examine (a) how well the coded data have addressed the research question, and (b) how well the coded material fits with and elaborates on the data set. Again, since coding in qualitative content analysis may be contextual and may draw on latent content, the creation of a transparent "map" to show readers how the codes were deductively created and applied is important. Sufficient raw data must be provided to the reader to illustrate in depth how coding was completed (Drisko, 2013b).

Combined Deductive and Inductive Coding

One limitation of deductive coding is that texts or newly collected data may contain important ideas or perspectives that were not previously identified in the conceptual and research literature. Researchers often discover points of view that arise from the comments of research participants. Still, the concepts and findings identified in the earlier literature may augment and help guide inductive qualitative content analyses in useful ways. Even where the literature is partial or does not include populations or topics of relevance to the current research question, the available literature may be conceptually useful. To make the best of both worlds, researches may use combinations of deductive and indicative coding in qualitative content analysis.

Employing a combined deductive–inductive coding plan requires that the researcher clearly explicate the sources of each kind of coding. How each category is developed and refined must be made transparent to the reader and illustrated with examples from the analysis. Steps used to ensure reliability and validity or trustworthiness and credibility must be clearly explained to the reader (Drisko, 2013b).

Validity and Reliability in Qualitative Content Analysis Coding

Much of the qualitative content analysis literature uses traditional, quantitative terminology to describe validity and reliability in coding. Consistency and agreement among coders are sought. For example, Mayring (2000) describes using the Cohen's kappa statistic. He states that a value of greater than .70 should be used to establish adequacy in inter-rater reliability. Coded text segments should also reflect the meaning of the categories to which the researchers assign them. Mayring (2000) also suggests triangulation as a useful technique to establish validity in qualitative content analysis. More recent qualitative concepts such as credibility, authenticity, and trustworthiness are not often found in this literature despite its qualitative orientation.

Schreier (2012, p. 16) argues that reliability is emphasized over validity in basic content analysis, while validity is emphasized in qualitative content analysis. This appears to be an exaggeration, as both validity and reliability (or their qualitative variants) should both be key factors in establishing rigor of any content analysis. The difference in emphasis may reflect the challenge of interpretive coding. In qualitative content analysis, a team of researchers must agree that content reflecting a category is present even when it is latent or implicit. The team serves as a set of peer reviewers of the quality and consistency of coding. Use of annotations and memos also helps with identifying and tracking questions and with areas lacking clarity. The team must agree that applying the code is valid, as is consistently applying the same code to varied but relevant content. In addition, the coded categories must be credible, authentic, and persuasive to readers of a qualitative content analysis.

To ensure reliability, pairs or teams of researchers often code the same textual material and compare their results. As in basic content analysis, discussion of the differences will initially serve to both identify areas of agreement and clarify differences in interpreting a segment of data. Initial training of research teams will improve coding consistency (reliability) and will improve the validity of coding. Mayring (2000) does not specifically mention such training, but his formative and summative reviews of the coded categories may serve similar functions.

Schreier (2012) suggests that triangulation with other data sources provides another technique to appraise the validity of qualitative content analyses. Indeed, George (1959a) reported that documents found after the end of World War II provided data that supported earlier interpretations of Nazi propaganda. The challenge to this method of establishing validity is that other sources of data are not always available or obvious. Member checks (reviewing data and researcher interpretations directly with the original research participants or the creators of texts under study) may not be possible when secondary data are used in content analysis.

Traditional methods of assessing validity and reliability may have limitations when used in qualitative content analysis. Chan et al. (2012) do not mention validity or reliability at all in their article. The authors do, however, identify several steps they took to ensure the trustworthiness of the data:

> Initially, multiple readings and open coding were conducted on all complete interview transcripts by three researchers; written memos on filial attitudes and behaviors on dignity were created, while codes were created to reflect the central characteristics of different narrative patterns. Second, [additional] coding was conducted to develop and refine possible categories of filial attitudes and behaviors, while text files containing illustrative and descriptive quotes supplementing the emergent themes were also created. Finally, three researchers independently reviewed and defined the emergent themes and presented to one another for confirmation; once consensus was reached, operational definitions were created. (p. 282)

The three researchers who agreed on the coding framework discussed and constantly compared how it addressed potential deviant cases during regular meetings. Such techniques may be viewed as promoting credibility and trustworthiness. Further clarification of how qualitative techniques ensure credibility and trustworthiness could strengthen the literature on qualitative content analysis methods.

DATA ANALYSIS IN QUALITATIVE CONTENT ANALYSIS

As a primarily descriptive research method, the process of coding encompasses a significant part of analysis in qualitative content analysis. Schreier (2014a) states that the main analysis is complete once the coding of the categories is finalized. She describes the final step of data analysis in qualitative content analysis as preparing the data in a manner that clearly answers the research question. This may involve developing a format of presentation that shows how the subunits of coded data collectively address the overall research question. Such an analysis will center on the reporting of descriptive categories or themes, together with illustrations of the evidence that supports the categories. Detailed description is the typical purpose of these analytic methods. Yet researchers can also use other methods of data presentation and re-presentation to analyze and report qualitative content analyses.

In a more general sense, the analysis phase of qualitative content analysis involves reorganizing and reordering the coded categories to summarize the key content in the data. Researchers undertake this reorganization to fully address the research question and reveal content of interest and importance to readers. There are several techniques for summarizing study data and organizing its presentation to readers (Krippendorff, 2013; Miles & Huberman, 1984).

Data Analysis and Presentation in Narrative Format

The most common form of presentation for qualitative content analysis studies is the use of a narrative format. In this form of analysis, the researchers identify core categories or themes and use these categories as section headings in the report. Each core theme is interpreted in a summary manner and illustrated using quotations that show how texts or participants portrayed their original ideas or views. This form of narrative analysis both clarifies how categories were developed and highlights categories that address the overall research question. The level of interpretation provided by the researchers may vary from minimal to significant. That is, categories or themes may merely be summarized to highlight the content, or the reader may be shown how more contextualized interpretations were made using latent content. Such contextualization may be as simple as showing how sarcasm or other figures of speech influence the meaning of a quotation. More complex interpretations of meaning and/or context may show how distinct quotations are related and shape meaning-making.

Chan et al. (2012) use a narrative approach to data analysis and presentation. One main theme in their end-of-life caregiver study, reciprocity in contemporary filial piety, is described as follows:

> Being able to discuss and share needs and concerns between parents and adult children in end-of-life caregiving was of paramount importance for sustaining filial conviction and behaviors. Janet, a 40-year-old daughter who supported her 83-year-old ailing mother through institutional care, said, "It is very important for me to talk to my mother openly about my difficulties with the care of my own family, and that I would not be able to take care of her at home. I had a great deal of regret because I knew that she didn't want to live in a nursing home, but she told me that it was fine and I was already doing the best that I could . . . I felt somewhat relieved knowing that she understood my situation and that I wasn't abandoning her. (p. 285)

In this passage, the researchers introduce the analytic theme of reciprocity and use it to summarize the content of the participant's statement. In all, three such quotations are provided to the reader. The passages show the reader how the theme summarizes the more detailed content of each original statement. Subjective experiences are captured using the overarching category, reciprocal relationships. Interpretation is minimal, though used to highlight the theme. The overall purpose of the qualitative content analysis remains essentially descriptive.

Narrative forms of data analysis and presentation in qualitative content analysis can be very persuasive. They may, however, be used selectively in ways that are not obvious to the reader. Researchers must take great care to *show* the reader that such quotations or text passages are typical of the entire data set. Narrative presentations may hide the impact of limited or selective sampling. To ensure rigor, iterative sampling must be undertaken to seek out potentially disconfirming participants or texts (Drisko, 1997, 2013b). Researchers should explicate such iterative efforts to the reader in the research report. Researchers should show the reader how extreme cases provide divergent or differently nuanced views on the research question. This both builds credibility or validity and helps the reader understand the applicability of study results and their limits. Similarly, presenting quotations or text passages that define the boundary conditions of a coded category or theme can help build credibility and point to views that do not fit with the bulk of the analysis. For example, a participant in the Chan et al. (2012) study might choose to follow the end-of-life wishes of his or her parent, maintaining a more traditional view of filial piety. The study shows readers one contemporary response to managing end-of-life caregiving but does not show that this is the most common or only way of understanding and managing this difficult situation. Researchers must be careful not to make overly sweeping claims based on small samples. Readers must always be critical readers of narrative analysis used in qualitative content analyses. Clear and thorough reporting shows the reader how the researchers sought to maintain rigor in their work.

Data Analysis and Presentation in Matrix Format

Comparison Tables

Miles and Huberman (1984; Miles, Huberman & Saldaña, 2014) note that comparison and contrast are useful methods of qualitative data analysis and display. When researchers use qualitative content analysis to address a comparative research question, charts and matrices may be useful methods of data analysis and presentation. These matrix displays may be used to compare texts or participants' responses within a single site or across sites in a tabular format. They may also be used to compare different texts or different sites examined in a single study. Miles and Huberman (1994, p. 79) state that matrix displays have several advantages over narrative presentations. Matrix displays (1) are concise rather than dispersed across several pages, (2) simultaneously present large amounts of data rather than presenting it sequentially, and (3) clearly order the data display. They are useful as a step in data analysis as well as for use in the final research report.

Flow Charts

Miles and Huberman (1984) note that flow charts describing complex processes can be another useful analytic and reporting technique. If the research question guiding a qualitative content analysis centers on examination of processes or events unfolding over time, a flow chart can clearly summarize key steps in such processes over time. Requisite conditions, decision points, and alternative outcomes may all be presented in a summary manner.

Matrix charts can also be used to show the effects of varying contexts. Different views or meanings that are reported or found in texts can be summarized in a context matrix. Such charts show how contexts influence meaning-making and action in a clear, descriptive fashion.

To date, the social work literature includes only a few matrix analyses and presentations of study data. These formats fit well with the page-length restrictions of most journal articles and can be a valuable analytic and presentation technique.

An Example of a Flow Chart and a Conceptual Diagram

Maschi, Baer, and Turner (2011) examined how social justice was integrated with clinical social work in published articles. Both "clinical social work" and "social justice" are widely used concepts of great importance to professional social work. Both terms are also difficult to delineate and are rarely defined fully in publications. The authors note that many earlier references to social justice and clinical social work are polemical, so a broader review of how these concepts were used in publications would be a valuable contribution to knowledge.

Drawing on a search of 59 online databases, a sample of 38 social work articles published between 1998 and 2009 that meet criteria were located. Maschi et al. found that only four articles in the sample included definitions of clinical social work, and only nine included definitions of social justice. Yet article authors identified both direct and indirect pathways through which social justice and clinical social work were integrated. These included the intersection of the psychological and sociopolitical environments, the use of integrative theories, and the use of specific strategies and practices.

To show readers how these publications portrayed the integration of clinical social work and social justice, Maschi et al. (2011) used both a flow chart and a conceptual diagram (see Figures 4.1 and 4.2). The

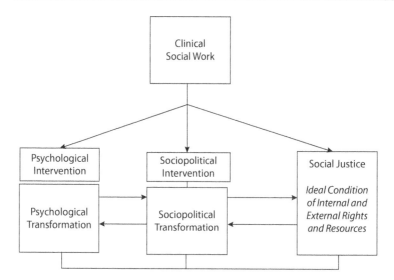

Figure 4.1. Flow chart describing direct and indirect integrative pathways. From Maschi, Bare, and Turner (2011, p. 238).

flow chart shows how the three pathways flow as distinct elements and as a whole. The researchers emphasized the interaction of the elements, effectively illustrating the complexity of the integration of clinical social work and social justice. All three key integrative pathways are summarized along with their interactions.

The conceptual diagram provides still more detail and scope (see Figure 4.2). The researchers show both the overarching context of clinical social work practice, including values and ethics, as influencing the social worker and the client in many ways. The conceptual diagram provides a larger perspective and more detail on specific interactions simultaneously. The researchers efficiently describe and summarize the multiple pathways of interaction for the reader.

Yang and Chen (2006) explored Chinese children's views on the meaning of death, using a qualitative content analysis. The 204 participants, ranging from fourth- to ninth-grade students at one high school in Taiwan, were each asked to complete a paragraph-length narrative on their views of death. The study sought to provide evidence on age-related variation in views on death, together with how life experiences of death shaped the narratives. The study drew on Piaget's developmental

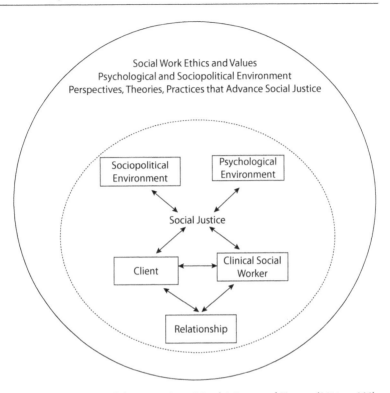

Figure 4.2. A conceptual diagram. From Maschi, Bare, and Turner (2011, p. 239).

framework and a theory of children's views of death that was developed by Neimeyer, Fontana, and Gold (1983) and Holcomb, Neimeyer, and Moore (1993). The participants were asked to write narratives using several prompts stated as sentence stems. The prompts included the following: "I think death is . . ."; "Reasons for death are . . ."; and "When I think about death, I will worry about or be afraid of . . ." (p. 221). The researchers also collected demographic data about family composition and death experiences.

Given the large data set and the prior conceptualization, a matrix of tabular presentation of data was used to summarize and describe the study findings. The matrix approach also ties short segments of raw data with each summary concept, helping readers understand the data that supported each key concept (see Table 4.1). The matrix identifies

Table 4.1. Matrix Presentation of Chinese Children's Views about Death (Partial)*

Category	Definition and examples	n (%)
1. Internal Causality	Some children attribute death to internal causality. Death may result from aging, sickness, and physical degeneration. • Death is caused by sickness, heart failure, or aging. • Death is caused by physical dysfunction.	153 (75%)
2. Negative Emotional State	When talking about death, some children show negative emotional states toward death, such as frustration, oppressiveness, grief, and sadness. • When I think about death, I am frustrated and down. It is painful and I'm scared. • When I think about death, I feel oppressed and I'm speechless.	142 (69.6%)
16. High Suffering	Some children mentioned that the process of death is painful or that death itself is the source of pain. • Death is painful. People die from diseases or in accidents. There are few chances to die naturally. Most people die in pain.	13 (6.37%)
17. Positive Valuation	Some children give a positive and active judgment toward death. They think that death is good and valuable and do not see it as terrible or scary. Such children thus can face death. • If there's heaven and hell, then I do not consider death a bad thing; I can meet my dead family members or friends there. • Death looks like lying down forever, just like going to sleep, and so it is not terrible. • Everyone will die, it is serious and dignified.	12 (5.88%)

*From Yang and Chen (2006, pp. 223–227).

each descriptive category, provides quotes from the participants, and provides a frequency statistic. In this way, researchers can convey to the reader information describing large data sets while including complex and subtly different raw data (Miles & Huberman, 1984; Miles et al., 2014).

Schreier (2012) states that using frequencies to report qualitative content analyses is helpful as these statistics show specifically how many participants or texts gave voice to each category or concept. This method is useful to orient the reader to findings from a large data set and to show the relative prevalence of each category. Of course, frequencies from small samples may not be transferable to other small samples nor reflect results that might be obtained from larger samples. Qualitative content analysts should clearly identify the limitations related to their samples when using frequency summaries. Using descriptively frequency statistics can be a valuable part of qualitative content analyses. Their limitation is that relative frequencies based on even 200 participants may not be representative of other, different samples or of the entire population. Yang and Chen (2006) sampled from one university-affiliated high school in Taiwan. This quite reasonable but a nonprobability sample does not allow quantitative generalization to all Chinese children of similar ages. The results, show, however, how prior concepts may be applied to these children and sensitize readers to questions to consider in their own settings. Frequencies should be used with caution in qualitative content analysis to avoid inappropriate overgeneralization from nonprobability samples.

Many analytic and data presentation techniques can be used in qualitative content analysis. Researchers can use both narrative and many different visual methods of data display to inform their readers. Visual techniques of data presentation can effectively summarize large and complex data sets and can illustrate complex interactions among data and concepts.

RESEARCHER SELF-REFLECTION AND REFLEXIVITY IN QUALITATIVE CONTENT ANALYSIS

Since the researcher is the instrument of coding and other analytic decisions in qualitative content analysis, self-reflection and reflexivity are important elements of the research process. Reflexivity in qualitative research addresses researcher engagement in explicit self-aware reviews of several kinds. These may range from individual self-awareness and self-reflection to intersubjective or collaborative processes to critical analyses. Finlay (2002) identifies five variants of reflexivity: (1) introspection, (2) intersubjective reflection, (3) mutual collaboration, (4) social critique, and (5) discursive deconstruction.

The purpose of self-reflection and reflexivity is to identify personal biases or viewpoints and larger social issues that may affect conceptual, methodological, and analytic decisions made during the project. Identifying such bias allows alterations in methods to address them or to account for them in other ways. It also informs the reader of areas in which the researcher's choices may warrant careful review. Finlay (2002, p. 215) notes: "The challenge for researchers using introspection is to use personal revelation not as an end in itself but as a springboard for interpretations and more general insight." That is, self-reflection is useful when it aids achievement of the overall research objectives. Such personal revelations may address intersubjective issues or more macro-level social critique.

There are no standards for researcher self-awareness or reflexivity in the current qualitative content analysis literature. This is in clear contrast to growing emphasis on both issues in qualitative research more generally. That said, without a standard or expectation for such reflection, it is typically lacking in qualitative content analysis reports.

For example, Maschi et al. (2011) discuss several potential limitations to their study but do not address reflexivity. Their identification of the limitations of their sample and cautions against overgeneralizations are clear and sound. They also note, with solid self-awareness, that other researchers might define different categories and that inter-rater reliability might be different with another team of researchers or data set. Wider reflexivity about power and context was not addressed.

Similarly, Chan et al. (2012, p. 293) state:

Despite their qualitative nature, the findings shed new light on the experience of family caregiving from the perspectives of adult-children caregivers, and carry important policy and clinical implications. In essence, the notion of filial piety has evolved in the contemporary context and now emphasizes reciprocal relationships, mutual support, and compassionate duty. However, the longstanding filial caregiving practice of task fulfillment has persisted, where the inability to provide practical and pragmatic care to parents at the end of life has caused shame and guilt among adult-children caregivers. Moreover, caregivers' sense of powerlessness to emotionally connect with their ailing parents has resulted in much regret and sorrow. These findings pinpoint the imperative for greater government assistance in home care support, as well as the critical need for a family-driven dignity-enhancing intervention in palliative social work.

These findings shed new light on filial piety in Chinese parental caregiving, but they may risk overgeneralization from a sample of 15 participants (3 male, 12 female). There is no caution to readers that these results should be viewed as pointing out new possibilities to be tested for applicability in other settings and with other caregivers. Chan et al. argue abductively for greater government assistance to support these caregivers, but they do not reflexively question the power structures in which they are embedded.

Most qualitative content analyses (like most interpretive content analyses) are "realist tales" (Van Maanen, 1983) in which the researcher does not engage in much formal self-reflection or reflexivity. Instead, interpretive content analyses emphasize unproblematized (more or less) objective "facts." Larger social contexts and power structures are rarely addressed as shaping study results, even speculatively. This perspective is consistent with positivist or realist epistemologies, but not with a constructivist epistemology or critical theory. Considerable additional work is needed to develop clarity regarding how choices of epistemology and techniques of self-reflection and reflexivity are applied in qualitative content analysis.

CHAPTER SUMMARY

Qualitative content analysis is a recent approach to content analysis that has strong potential for social work research. The new approach is still developing, and the literature is sometimes contradictory on both general research methods and specific techniques. Qualitative content analysis may be framed inductively, deductively, or using a combination of both approaches. It is a flexible research method (Anastas, 1999). Qualitative content analysis may use either newly collected data, existing texts and materials, or a combination of both. It may be used in exploratory, descriptive, comparative, or explanatory research designs, though its primary use is descriptive.

Many techniques of coding data are now discussed in the qualitative content analysis literature, though further elaboration and clarification of these techniques are needed. Although most analyses use narrative data analysis and presentation techniques, other methods are also found in the current literature. These include flow charts, conceptual diagrams, and tabular charts summarizing study analyses. Additional examination of the role of epistemology and of sampling methods is needed to ensure rigor in qualitative content analysis. The iterative cycle of sampling, data collection, and data analysis can be a valuable part of strengthening qualitative content analysis methods. Steps toward including potentially disconfirming data will also improve the rigor of qualitative content analyses. Further exploration of the appropriate role of abductive claims made using qualitative content analysis results is also warranted.

Qualitative content analysis appears to be very similar to some other models of qualitative research. These include Boyatzis' (1998) thematic analysis and Hill's (2011) consensual qualitative research. Qualitative content analysis is also quite different from some other qualitative research methods. The coding process of qualitative content analysis may initially be similar to the coding processes developed for grounded theory, but description rather than development of mid-level theory is the research objective (Glaser & Strauss, 1967). Qualitative content analyses typically use a single-stage method of data analysis, while grounded theory uses a three-stage, iterative method. In contrast to discourse analysis, qualitative content analysis focuses more on content than on discourse process, may be based on positivist/realist epistemologies rather than solely on a constructivist epistemology, and is much less likely to include critical analyses (Schreier, 2012). In contrast to semiotic analysis, qualitative content analysis is more descriptive and is much less likely to include critical interrogation of the data (Schreier, 2012). Researchers need to more clearly identify the unique aspects of qualitative content analysis.

5

Enhancing Rigor in Content Analysis Studies and Reports

This chapter examines the steps that researchers should undertake to ensure rigor in their studies and reports. The chapter opens with a section that applies to all three types of content analyses—basic, interpretive, and qualitative. The chapter ends with sections differentiated by approach to content analysis when steps to ensure rigor diverge.

COMMON STEPS TO ENSURE RIGOR ACROSS CONTENT ANALYSIS APPROACHES

We view rigor as involving both application of appropriate techniques and research methods and application of such methods in an internally consistent manner to achieve the study objectives (Drisko, 1997, 2013b). Researchers should make choices that frame a coherent and internally consistent study. Researchers should also clearly inform their readers of these choices.

Starting with a Research Question of Merit and Worth

First, writing up and reporting a content analysis study begins with a clear statement of the research question. Researchers should make clear to readers both what the analysis will contribute to knowledge and how it will influence professional thinking and practice. It is also useful to describe the intended audience for the study, although in practice this is mainly done implicitly. The objective of these statements is to locate the reader and clarify the purposes of the study. Methods should then be applied that achieve the purposes of the study.

Identifying the Selected Study Epistemology

Researchers should then state the epistemology used to orient the study. Such statements are rare in publications by researchers applying positivist or realist epistemologies. They are common by researchers applying a constructivist epistemology, though hardly universal. The purpose of such statements is to help the reader understand the premises of the study: a single consensus way of knowing or multiple and potentially diverse ways of knowing. Epistemological choices have important consequences for rigor in methods, analysis, and reporting. Such choices help shape the application of different standards for reliability or validity, versus verisimilitude, credibility, and transferability. Several scholars argue that quantitative methods for enhancing reliability and validity may not fit well with a multiple ways of knowing epistemology (Denzin & Lincoln, 2005; Guba & Lincoln, 1989; Polkinghorne, 1988).

Ensuring Appropriate Research Ethics and Participant Safeguards

Researchers also need to clearly state all steps taken to ensure the protection of human research participants. This may require only a sentence or two, but it makes clear to the reader that the researchers appropriately considered the privacy and dignity of their participants and participants' right to informed consent. When electronic data are used, an explanation of how consent was obtained (as appropriate) and how participants' privacy was protected is also warranted. A statement of institutional review board approval should be part of all studies for which it is applicable. However, no such statement may be required when texts or other materials in the public domain are the sole source of data for a content analysis.

Stating the Study Research Design

Researchers should state the research design of the study clearly. Students and experienced researchers often find the distinction between exploratory and descriptive research to be murky. In fact, many content analyses are both exploratory and descriptive simultaneously. That is, they provide new information about texts or groups that researchers had never included in prior studies or included in prior studies of a specific topic. In this sense, most content analyses are at least partly exploratory in design. The vast majority of content analyses are also descriptive in research design in that they document the characteristics of a specific sample of texts or participants on a specific issue. Yet some content analyses appear to be comparative, predictive, or explanatory in design and purpose. Researchers should also clearly inform their readers about how the chosen research design supports development of an evidence base appropriate to the overall study question(s).

DIFFERENTIATED STEPS TO ENSURE RIGOR BY CONTENT ANALYSIS APPROACH

At this point, somewhat different steps are required to support the rigor of each of the three approaches to content analysis. The impact of different research purposes and epistemological choices will shape methodological choices regarding sampling, data collection, data analysis, and the reporting of study findings.

Clarifying the Characteristics of the Sample

The nature of the sample should be clearly explicated. Researchers undertaking content analyses employ many different sampling techniques. How the chosen sampling plan provides appropriate evidence for answering the study question(s) should be explained to the reader. The nature of the sample will also shape the appropriate use of some analytic methods. Researchers should also explain if and how the chosen sample size supports generalizations or transferability across people and settings. Transparent statements of the characteristics of the sample are crucial to establishing the potential replication of any content analysis.

Strengthening Sampling in Basic Content Analysis
Researchers should give careful thought to the connection between the sample of a basic content analysis and its later impact on the appropriate use of statistics. The use of parametric statistics will often require use of a probability sample, giving each case in the population equal chance of selection. Such statistics are not appropriate to apply to nonprobability samples. Krippendorff (2013) also reminds researchers that the independence of the elements within a sample in basic content analysis is often compromised. Establishing the independence of elements to be compared with each other or that will be used as grouping variables is important in order to meet the assumptions of some inferential statistics. Further, specific sample sizes may also be required to ensure the statistical power of the researcher's selected analysis (Dattalo, 2008).

Strengthening Sampling in Interpretive and Qualitative Content Analysis
As noted in Chapters 3 and 4, sampling in interpretive and qualitative content analysis is a minimally addressed topic in the literature; there is considerable room for further elaboration and clarification of the role of sampling with each content analysis method. This makes attention to sampling an important step in ensuring the rigor of interpretive and qualitative content analyses.

Researchers undertaking most interpretive and qualitative content analyses use purposive samples. That is, texts or participants are selected to provide plentiful relevant information for the study. It is indeed important that such samples be maximally informative. The risk is that even large purposive samples may represent only a few viewpoints and may not provide a range of meanings. Whether premised on positivist/realist or constructivist epistemologies, interpretive and qualitative content analyses must provide a variety of viewpoints and social positions. To fail to do so can amount to gathering a set of similar texts while ignoring other views and ways of understanding.

To ensure rigor, use of iterative sampling that researchers actively revise on the basis of preliminary findings is preferable to a single-stage sample technique. The purpose of this iterative revision of the sample is to identify texts or participants who might give divergent views and perspectives and to take steps to include them actively in the study sample. Sampling techniques such as maximum variation sampling and extreme case sampling are used to include a range of viewpoints in the sample. Such sampling techniques can help realize the goal of purposefully gathering the potential views found in texts or stated by research participants. The aim of these techniques is to counter claims that the sample was homogenous or potentially limited in representing potential views and meanings. Seeking out potentially contradictory and/or clarifying data should always be part of sampling in interpretive or qualitative content analysis.

Detailing the Data Collection Methods

Researchers should also fully explain the data collection methods used in a content analysis study. For some content analyses, this will center on the choice of specific texts and passages within these texts. Texts may include books, newspapers, professional journal articles, public documents such as program descriptions, images, ads, photos, videos, audio recordings, and many forms of electronic media. For other content analyses, interviews and short written narratives are the data source. In some content analysts, computer-assisted data collection is undertaken using specific dictionaries of search terms and automated coding (e.g., Gottschalk, 1995).

Researchers should make clear to the reader how and why data are chosen and collected. How these data serve as an appropriate and comprehensive evidence base for later conclusions should be clearly explained. Transparent and thorough explication of the data collection is also vital to potentially replication any content analysis.

Detailing Coding and Data Analysis

Researchers should always describe their coding and data analysis in detail. Whether researchers develop code lists a priori and deductively, or inductively during analysis, or use a mix of both approaches, this choice must be stated. Steps taken to train coders and any other steps taken to ensure the reliability of the coded data should be described thoroughly. When computer-assisted coding is used, the nature of the dictionary of codes and the algorithm for data collection should be explained in detail.

Strengthening Coding and Analysis in Basic Content Analysis
Basic content analyses typically use a priori code lists or use a mix of a priori and inductively developed codes that address content that the original code list did not adequately cover. Basic content analysts should either include the full coding list in their reports or make clear how readers may access the full coding list. Such codes lists, also called dictionaries, may be copyrighted; therefore, access to the authors or publishers may be restricted or require payment. Readers should be informed transparently how they may access complete code lists.

Some code lists are reported in full via a list of key findings or themes. When codes are used in the analysis but are not reported, researchers should explain why they did not apply these codes. This gives the reader an opportunity to learn what codes did not successfully apply to a specific set of data, based on a defined sample. In such instances both positive findings (instances of code use) and negative findings (codes that did not prove useable) are informative.

Researchers should describe efforts to train coders and to enhance and document inter-coder reliability in full. Several methods to assess inter-rater reliability are described in Chapter 2 and in other resources (e.g., Krippendorff, 2013). Such efforts typically improve coding consistency and allow discussion and elaboration of any codes or texts that may be ambiguous. Similarly, any computer software or algorithms used to create word counts or to code texts should be described in detail. Computer-aided analyses have the advantage of reliability and thoroughness, but they are only as good as the code lists and instructions that orient them. (Neuendorf [2007] offers a valuable online listing of computer programs for content analysis.)

Researchers using statistical analysis methods must explain in detail how they applied all descriptive or inferential statistics. Researchers should show how the chosen statistics meet any limiting assumptions for use of the statistics (such as appropriate levels of measures and requirements for probability samples). As appropriate, sample sizes should be adequate to provide necessary power to demonstrate statistical significance (Dattalo, 2008).

Strengthening Coding and Analysis in Interpretive and Qualitative Content Analyses

Since both interpretive and qualitative content analyses typically make use of inductive coding methods, researchers should provide multiple examples of how they made coding decisions. Providing several examples of raw data, and how and why it was coded in a specific manner, *shows* the reader how coding was undertaken. Readers should be provided with or give instructions on how they may obtain the full list of codes used in the study. This would allow for replication of a given content analysis by other researchers.

Because latent or context-sensitive materials may be coded and analyzed in interpretive and qualitative content analyses, sufficient raw data should be made available for the reader to understand and interrogate the researcher's decisions. Several passages of text should be presented verbatim (or as collected) to orient the reader to the content and context. Next, the researcher should show the reader how coding was done, clearly linking specific data to code names. This is most often undertaken using a narrative reporting method, providing readers with text, context as appropriate, and an explanation of why the code was applied.

Including some examples of text passages that the researchers considered for coding with a specific code name but ultimately were not coded with that name further shows the reader the boundaries of the process. Most interpretive and qualitative content analyses provide readers with examples that solely affirm the study conclusions but fail to show how the researchers sought out and understood potentially disconfirming or divergent material. Credibility is enhanced when readers can see that the researchers did not simply "line up" supporting evidence. Where context shapes meaning (e.g., sarcasm or irony), the researcher should provide sufficient raw data to show the impact of context on meaning. If it is not possible to show the reader how context shapes meaning, an additional explanatory statement from the researcher is indicated. For example, the researcher must explain how they interpreted passages of text in which expression and intonation influenced meaning. Researchers cannot easily convey such enacted aspects of communication in print text, but they can do this quite clearly in audio or video recordings. Where possible, researchers should make raw data available in forms that include such enacted, contextual factors.

Researchers should show how all descriptive summaries are linked to the collected data. Readers should find such connections transparent and replicable. This expectation is widely stated in the content analysis literature (Krippendorff, 2013, Schreier, 2012).

Researcher Self-Reflection and Reflexivity

In qualitative content analyses, researcher should address self-reflection and/or reflexivity. The researcher should briefly state any biases or initial expectations that influenced the study question, data collection, and data analysis. Descriptions of coding and analysis should explicate how multiple standpoints and other contextual influences impact the interpretation of meaning in the data. This expectation is increasingly common in qualitative research based on a constructivist epistemology or on critical/normative theories.

DISCUSSING RESULTS

Content analysis is most often a form of descriptive research. Researchers must take care to keep their conclusions closely connected to the collected and reported data.

Krippendorff (2013) points out that many content analysts make abductive interpretations from their study results. Abductive arguments link an observation with a hypothesis that accounts for or potentially explains the observation (Reichertz, 2014). However, abductive reasoning does not guarantee the correctness of the conclusion. It is an inference only to a plausible or possible explanation. Additional sources of supporting evidence must be triangulated with the content analysis results to further validity and abductive claim (Krippendorff, 2013). While researchers use content analyses to makes claims that there is "too little" or "too much" content on a topic, the actual empirical data rarely address these claims directly. Researchers should be careful not to overstate content analysis results supporting normative claims without having additional validating evidence.

RIGOR: MAINTAINING THE INTERNAL CONSISTENCY OF THE STUDY

All content analysis reports should be internally consistent. That is, a report based on a constructivist epistemology should not shift into the use of terminology and techniques based on positivist or realist epistemologies. Further, generalizing to populations from small purposeful samples would seem inconsistent with a constructivist epistemology. So, too, generalizing to entire populations from nonprobability samples would be inconsistent with a positivist or realist epistemology, as well as a poor fit with the chosen sampling plan.

Discussions and implications should be limited to the examined data or appropriate abductive inferences from it. Content analysis can provide a useful evidence base for many forms of advocacy, but it may not always point to just one answer. For instance, a content analysis of qualitative research content in MSW foundation research courses can describe what is typically taught, but it does not automatically indicate that this content is "too little" or "too much." Researchers must take care to show additional supporting evidence in making abductive inferences from content analysis findings.

6

Content Analysis for Public Awareness and Advocacy

Over the past 100 years, social work has grown from the industrial countries of the United States and England and spread to the villages and cities, large and small, and to all corners of the globe (Sowers & Rowe, 2007). With this expansion, the field of international social work has grown. International social work is referred to as "international professional action" by social workers (Healey, 2001, p. 7). These activities include international practice, policy development, and research and evaluation with an increasing emphasis on addressing human rights violations and social injustices committed "close to home," such as mass incarceration, especially of racial/ethnic minorities and other vulnerable populations, in the United States (Sowers & Rowe, 2007; Tripodi & Potocky-Tripodi, 2007).

Social work professionals are a powerful and collective force in efforts to effectively prevent or alleviate adverse social conditions. Poverty, child abuse, HIV/AIDS, substance abuse, crime, and the structural oppression of women, persons of color, and individuals with physical and mental health disabilities are just some of the areas where social workers have an impact (Sowers & Rowe, 2007). Similar to social work forefathers and foremothers, contemporary social workers can conduct community-based research and apply these strategies at the grassroots level in their local communities or abroad (Austin, 2003; Zimbalist, 1977). The use of content analysis methods of newly collected or existing data along with an action plan can play an instrumental role in shedding light on undetected social problems. Content analysis methods can also be used as part of a data analysis plan to evaluate practices, programs, policies, and laws.

Social workers are involved in national and international social work research efforts. Using a "single-country perspective," domestic social work researchers examine the population of one country, such as the United States. Only the literature of one country is used to frame the social problem, conduct the study, and apply the findings. A large majority of American social work research, for instance, is conducted in the United States for the U.S. population. In international social work research, by contrast, the efforts extend beyond a country's borders to investigate social problems and solutions in other countries (Tripodi & Potocky-Tripodi, 2007). Regardless of the geographic focus, content analysis methods offer a versatile approach that social work researchers can use when deciding on a data analysis plan involving quantitative and/or qualitative methods, with the goal of building public awareness and practice and policy reform.

To this end, this chapter reviews how content analysis approaches can be used in efforts to increase public awareness and advocacy in the promotion of human rights and social justice for historically and emerging underrepresented and underserved populations at local and global levels. As reviewed in Chapters 1–5, results from content analysis methods often have been used to provide valuable empirical evidence for addressing contemporary social problems such as healthcare, social welfare, and juvenile and criminal justice reform. In the new era of competency-based social work education which mandates that social workers be prepared to engage in practices advocating for human rights and social justice, social work research and evaluation also needs to follow suit. This chapter outlines how content analysis results can be used in a human rights–based strategy for building public awareness and advocacy, from problem formulation to dissemination of information and taking action.

Figure 6.1 illustrates the research cycle applied to the content analysis process that incorporates social and behavioral change. The process starts with the initial stage of identifying the social problem then proceeds to developing research questions and/or hypotheses, choosing a sample and data collection procedures, analyzing results, sharing the findings, and taking action. For social workers to be true to their mission of advancing human rights and social and economic justice, phases of the research process need to be examined using a human rights and social justice lens.

For a more detailed description of research using a human rights and social justice framework, see Maschi (2010a) and Wronka (2007). For the purposes of public awareness and advocacy, content analysis findings should be designed to include dissemination of findings and action planning that go beyond the academic community to reach the general public. When research findings reach society at large, citizens then have the chance to use these findings in a collective decision-making

Figure 6.1. An action oriented research cycle applied to the content analysis process.

process toward achieving a more just and equitable society. Social workers may get their "message" out by publishing white papers, reports, and peer-reviewed journal articles. They can also make presentations to community members or policymakers and use social media, such as writing op-ed pieces and blogs (Ife, 2001a, 2001b; Reichert, 2003; United Nations [UN], 1994; Wronka, 2007).

CRITICAL REFLECTION

We recommend that social workers who conduct research and evaluation studies, including content analysis literature review projects, explore how their own socioeconomic positions of power and privilege differ in relation to those of the populations they are studying. Social workers also need to evaluate how their research problem is positioned in the sociopolitical context. Some scholars and practitioners speak to the importance of critical self-reflection in the form of self-awareness and self-evaluation (Singer, 2006). Reeser (2009) has offered some helpful critical analysis strategies for social workers that can be applied in the context of research practice. These are summarized next.

- *Awareness of the political nature of practice.* Social workers should be aware that there is a political aspect of social work practice, including research and evaluation. Garnering a vision of a just society will help promote social justice, human rights, and well-being among all individuals, both locally and globally.
- *Engagement in self-reflection and action.* Social workers should engage in thoughtful reflection and action in their work. This involves engaging in critical self-reflection and reexamining one's socioeconomic position (e.g., race, class, gender, and class) and how it is linked to the larger environmental context.
- *Awareness of the personal-is-political connection.* Social workers should be aware of the connection between personal experience and actions and related political effects. This awareness helps remind social workers of the connection between the individual and the larger sociopolitical context.
- *Awareness of top-down strategies.* Social workers should be aware of top-down strategies—that is, strategies used by the

status quo (e.g., those that hold power) to maintain power and control, and strategies that advance equity and fairness.

- *Awareness of bottom-up change in power.* Social workers also need to be aware of how power can be changed from the "bottom up." That is, the rank and file has the power to change unjust structures. Social workers should be committed to empowering people to recognize and use their resources. Front-line social workers also can realize the impact of building data from the ground up, which can help move the profession forward (Reeser, 2009).

CONTENT ANALYSIS AND PUBLIC AWARENESS CAMPAIGNS

Researchers can use content analysis methods and results to engage key stakeholders, build networks and support, increase public awareness, foster collective dialogue and debate, and advance advocacy efforts (Centre for Civil Society, 2003). A publication awareness campaign is an important aspect of diffusing innovative research findings that may affect public opinion and social and behavioral change among the general public. If research findings reach the general public, there is a heightened chance that these findings may influence the development, modification, and implementation of practices and policies that have a beneficial impact on all citizens. The main objectives of public awareness campaigns are to draw the public's attention to certain public issues or problem areas and to bring about behavior and social change. When attempting to communicate innovative ideas and research findings, it is important to consider the targeted audience or audiences who are affected so that they understand and accept the message (Wronka, 2007).

Advocacy for a cause often goes hand in hand with a campaign to build public awareness. *Advocacy* generally refers to "the act of directly representing, defending, intervening, supporting, or recommending a course of action on behalf of one or more individuals, groups, or communities with the goal of securing or retaining social justice" (Mickelson, 1995, p. 95). At a minimum, the results of content analysis methods should include a discussion of the implications and recommendations for practice and policy reform that advocates in the field can use and for future directions for research. In other cases, research findings may be incorporated into an advocacy campaign. Table 6.1 provides examples of possible venues and strategies to share research findings for public awareness and advocacy.

Table 6.1. Possible Venues and Strategies to Share Research Findings for Public Awareness and Advocacy

Potential Actions to Share Findings	Possible Venues	Examples of Activities
Write	Publications	Publish peer-reviewed research or practice in journals Publish books or book chapters in area of expertise
Present	Professional research conferences— international, national, regional	Oral presentation Roundtable discussion Poster presentation Workshop Political meetings
Broadcast	Internet	Your own or an organization's website
	Email	Email newsletters, Twitter, Facebook
	Television or radio (local, national/international)	Press release, documentary, news item, interview
	Magazines, newspaper (local, national/ international)	Op-ed piece, editorial, letter to editor, blog, press release
Attend events	Professional practice conferences— international, national, local	Do a workshop or presentation
Advocate	Political events Charity events Public forums Town hall meetings Court hearings Other community events	Use research for advocacy
Network	Community stakeholders	Build coalitions, cross-sectoral collaborations for practice and policy reform

CONTENT ANALYSIS AND ADVOCACY

Social workers often engage in advocacy with and on behalf of historical underrepresented and underserved populations, such as individuals and families living in poverty, racial/ethnic minorities, women and children, and the incarcerated and formerly incarcerated. Dalrymple and Boylan (2013) describe two types of advocacy strategies that social workers use: case- or issue-based advocacy, and systemic or cause advocacy. In case-based advocacy, social workers often work with individuals or families in the context of their day-to-day practice. Systemic advocacy, in contrast, often refers to interventions to change the environment through social policy. Social workers who engage in systemic advocacy use the practice knowledge gained from individual cases for collective advocacy in order to work toward systemic changes in legislation, policy, and practice. Basic, interpretive, and qualitative findings based on content analyses of individual case-level data can be a powerful tool in identifying the frequency of occurrence of service use patterns and common themes experienced among service users and providers. These may include the barriers and facilitators to gaining access to services or the impact of policies (or lack thereof) that affects individual, family, and community health and well-being.

Another way to view advocacy is in both passive and active forms. In a passive form of advocacy the focus is on service users or clients requiring service provision and protections. In active advocacy service users are viewed as active citizens and participants. Thus, *passive advocacy* refers to an advocate speaking and acting on behalf of a client population, while *active advocacy* refers to a person or group speaking and acting on their own behalf (Dalrymple & Boylan, 2013). Social workers engaging in research may use their content analysis findings through advocacy on a social justice issue on behalf of those most affected by it. They also may work with advocates or advocacy organizations of individuals affected by an issue who can use their published results as part of their public awareness or advocacy campaigns.

Content analysis findings often provide a succinct overview of a large body of literature and can highlight that research, practice, and policy gaps and/or expose a critical social issue and provide recommendations for policy reform and advocacy. For example, child maltreatment was not always considered a social problem. In fact, the "discovery" of child maltreatment, in 1962, was the result of a group of radiologists and doctors identifying and documenting the frequency and occurrence of visual signs of physical abuse, such as the broken bones and fractures, in infants and children during medical examinations. Dr. Kempe's naming of the "battered child syndrome" put a face on the once-hidden social problem of child abuse (Kempe, Silverman, Steele, Droegemueller, & Silver, 1962). The research that followed and the work of child advocates eventually made child maltreatment an illegal act with the 1974 federal passage of the Child Abuse Prevention Act (Finkelhor, Cross, & Cantor, 2005).

A more contemporary social issue is the growing awareness of the problem of aging, seriously ill, and dying people in prison, especially in the United States. Recent civil and human right reports and a growing body of research findings, including a content analysis of the literature, have been a very effective tool for building awareness and policy advocacy (e.g., American Civil Liberties Union (ACLU), 2012; Human Rights Watch (HRW), 2012, Maschi, Viola, & Sun, 2013). When presented with mounting research evidence, the general public and policymakers are more likely to recognize and respond to the issue at hand (Mayer, 2009). The following detailed abstract on palliative and end-of-life care in prisons by Maschi, Marmo, and Han (2014) describes the background of the problem; the content analysis process and results; and the research, practice, and social implications. Additionally, Chapter 7 provides an example of content analysis methods of primary data on older adults' traumatic and stressful experiences of prison.

Purpose: The growing number of terminally ill and dying persons in prison has high economic and moral costs in global correctional systems and for society at large. However, little is known about the extent to which palliative and end-of-life care is used within global prison healthcare systems. The purpose of this study is to fill a gap in the literature by reviewing and critically appraising the methods and major findings of the international peer-reviewed literature on palliative and end-of-life care in prisons, identifying the common elements of promising palliative and end-of-life services in prison, and identifying the factors that facilitate or create barriers to implementation.

Design/methodology/approach: A content analysis was conducted of the existing peer-reviewed literature on palliative and end-of-life care in prison. English-language articles were located through a comprehensive search of peer-reviewed journals, such as Academic Search Premier Literature databases, using various combinations of keyword search terms, such as "prison," "palliative care," and "end-of-life care." A total of 49 studies published between 1991 and 2013 met criteria for sample inclusion. Deductive and inductive analysis techniques were used to generate frequency counts and common themes related to the methods and major findings.

Findings: The majority ($N = 39$) of studies were published between 2001 and 2013, in the United States ($n = 40$) and the UK ($n = 7$). Most were about U.S. prison hospice programs ($n = 16$) or barriers to providing palliative and end-of-life care in prisons ($n = 10$). The results of the inductive analysis identified common elements of promising practices, which included the use of peer volunteers, multidisciplinary teams, staff training, and partnerships with community hospices. Factors identified as obstacles to infusing palliative and end-of-life care in prisons included ethical dilemmas based on custody versus care; mistrust between staff and prisoners; safety concerns; concern about prisoners' potential misuse of pain medication; and institutional, staff, and public apathy toward terminally ill prisoners and their human right to health in the form of compassionate and palliative care, including the use of compassionate release laws.

Research limitations/implications: Implications for future research include fostering of prisoners' human rights and of public awareness of the economic and moral costs of housing the sick and dying in prisons. More research is needed to document human rights violations as well as best practices and evidence-based practices in palliative and end-of-life care in prisons. Future studies should incorporate data from the terminally ill in prison, peer supports, and family members. Future studies should also employ more rigorous research designs to evaluate human rights violations, staff and public attitudes, laws and policies, and best practices. Quantitative studies using experimental designs, longitudinal data, and multiple informants are needed. Qualitative data would enable thick descriptions of key stakeholders' experiences, especially of the facilitators, and of barriers to implementing policy reform efforts and palliative care in prisons.

Practical implications: This review provides a foundation to build on regarding what is known about the human right to health, especially parole policy reform and the use of palliative and end-of-life care for terminally ill and dying persons in prisons. This information can be used to develop or improve a new generation of research, practice, policy, and advocacy efforts targeting those who are terminally ill and dying in prison, and their families and communities.

Social implications: There are significant social implications to this review. From a human rights perspective, the right to freedom from torture and cruel and unusual punishment is a fundamental human right, along with prisoners' right to an appropriate level of healthcare. These rights should be guaranteed regardless of the nature of their crime or whether they are in prison. The information provided in this review can be used to educate and possibly transform individuals' and society's views toward the terminally ill and dying who are in the criminal justice system.

Application

In order to use content analysis methods and findings for advocacy, social workers need to understand the situation, policies, public perception, client–environment intervention, and other issues related to the problem (Mayer, 2009). These various positions may necessitate different advocacy responses (Kuji-Shakatani, 2004). Case-level advocacy efforts may resemble case management, such as advocating for needed resources or basic human rights, for example, access to housing, employment, and healthcare. Social workers may also engage in systemic-level advocacy as political advocates. Critical communication can occur between case-level advocates who are privy to information from the grass roots level about a client population. This information can be shared with policy-level advocates who, in turn, can share this information with policymakers. Policy advocates in return can provide case advocates with critical information on laws, policies, and potential service loopholes so that they can best help their clients (Mickelson, 1995).

Social workers can assist advocates in the field. This assistance might include a content analysis of legislative records on a targeted policy or legal issue, such as public records of legislative hearings regarding gun laws, healthcare legislation, or organizational case records. Content analysis findings can be a powerful advocacy tool, because they give a palatable overview of a content area that relevant agency administrators and public policymakers require as evidence on which to base their decisions (Reisch, 2009). This shift from conducting research to advocacy often lies with the social worker's ability to effectively communicate this information to key stakeholders using oral or written communication that the general public can easily understand (Chataway, Joffe, & Mordaunt, 2009).

Content analysis methods used with primary or secondary data can significantly raise public awareness, including that of public administrators, policymakers, and advocacy groups. In fact, many organizational, political, and advocacy leaders are open to consulting with experts, including researchers with knowledge about a given social problem or population. If community and organizational leadership and staff are well versed in the empirical evidence and their local population profile, they are best prepared to support their advocacy efforts with empirical evidence (Chataway et al., 2009; Mayer, 2009). Social workers can use content analysis methods to synthesize available evidence, including an analysis of newspaper articles and legislative and public records, which can be used to educate about and advocate for social and political positions.

CONTENT ANALYSIS AND GLOBAL RESEARCH AND EVIDENCE-BASED POLICYMAKING

Content analysis results can be used to raise local to global public awareness and to promote advocacy at the supranational (beyond borders), intranational (within borders), and transnational (across borders) (Tripodi & Potocky-Tripodi, 2007). Since supranational research is most concerned with research and populations beyond one's country's borders, content analysis strategies can be used with primary and secondary data collected in other countries. In contrast to domestic research, *supranational* research uses empirical evidence, including the research literature, from two or more countries to frame research problems, design research studies, and draw implications based on the findings from two or more countries. In contrast, *intranational* research is conducted within one country's borders with immigrant populations. Intranational research uses the literature from the country of origin and country of emigration to frame research problems. Implications are drawn for both countries. Transnational research differs from the other types in that it is conducted across national borders. *Transnational* research consists of comparative research using similar populations in two or more countries. The literature across the different countries' populations is used to frame research problems. Implications are drawn across each population (Tripodi & Potocky-Tripodi, 2007). Content analysis methods used with any of these three types of international research methods can be used to examine within- and between-group differences using the total population or subpopulation groups of one or more countries.

Global evidence-based policy is of growing interest among key stakeholder groups, including policymakers and advocacy groups (Thomas & Mohan, 2007). Content analysis methods can also play a role in the analysis of local, national, or international policies and research evidence as well as primary data collected from key stakeholders in the field. Similar to evidence-based practice, evidence-based policymaking draws on the best available evidence and knowledge to develop or improve policies with the aim of having a therapeutic effect on the health and well-being of all individuals, families, and communities (Mayer, 2009). However, there are some challenges to using evidence-based policymaking. First, there is not always evidence available to make policy decisions. Second, there are serious issues of legitimacy and power relations at an international level if Western ways of knowing that revere logic and rationality and status of experts are the central frameworks used. Therefore, alternative ways of knowing relevant to underrepresented and underserved populations often hold very little weight in policy debates unless there is a strong collective advocacy response.

In reality, evidence-based policymaking is complex when implemented in the field (Mayer, 2009). Mayer (2009) has recommended strategies for improving the quality of research and its effectiveness in changing public policy and public action. One must think critically about problems in advance and propose methods to use before acting. Careful reflection can assist with conceptualizing the central issues and assessing the feasibility of the research and the data sources needed to provide evidence. Content analysis is a useful tool that social work researchers can draw on because it can be applied to primary and secondary data collection and analysis to formulate an action plan. However, the use of empirical evidence will not always result in a shift in public opinion or behavior. Thus, an important strategy is to talk about content analysis findings realistically in the advocacy arena; that is, avoid talking about results as if they "prove" something. This assertion makes it easy for others to attack since all research results are to some degree inconclusive (Mayer, 2009).

Communication Strategies

For social work researchers who engage in policy advocacy, part of the strategy is to use evidence to motivate or persuade others to recognize and respond to social problems, such as the plight of maltreated children and elders. Researchers equipped with the knowledge and skills of persuasive communication are in an advantageous position to use their research findings to build an evidence base for social change. Persuasive written or oral communication consists of three key ingredients—ethos, logos, and pathos—that a researcher can use to promote an action-based research agenda (Wronka, 2007).

Since content analysis results are often disseminated in white papers or reports, research briefs, and/or peer-reviewed journal articles, the following discussion concerns written communication.

The first ingredient, *ethos*, refers to a writer's recognized authority to write about a particular topic. A person with authority may be a social work scholar or academic expert, a seasoned practitioner, and/or an advocate. In some cases, the person with authority may be a social worker who also has the "lived experience" of a social issue, such as being a child survivor of abuse and neglect, reflecting both a personal and professional level of expertise.

The second persuasive communication ingredient, *logos*, commonly reinforces ethos because the person with authority uses evidence and reason as part of their communication strategy. Evidence may include the presentation of factual data and statistics, including the results of a content analysis, as a strategy to educate and persuade others. For example, logos mostly describes the use of evidence to support an important point. One example may be providing background to a problem, such as local, national, and international statistics of the prevalence and incidence of child maltreatment or elder abuse. Content analysis findings based on current research findings may be used to identify characteristics of the causes, correlates, and consequences of child maltreatment, or an analysis of the literature might be used. It is important to note that sharing information with the general public should be reader-friendly and the use of jargon minimized.

The third persuasive communication strategy, *pathos*, appeals more to emotions than to reason. Social work researchers can achieve pathos as a passionate delivery that moves beyond connecting with their audience through intellect and emotions to motivating them to action.

The challenge for researchers is integrating ethos, logos, and pathos successfully to make an argument persuasive to a given audience (Aristotle, 350 BC/2000; Wisse, 1989). Researchers can use a combination of basic, interpretive, and/or qualitative approaches to content analysis to build awareness and incorporate it into their public awareness and advocacy efforts. The result of successful messaging can in turn lead to actions taken to improve social conditions for individuals, families, and communities at the local, national, and global levels (Thomas & Mohan, 2007).

Social work researchers should also be aware that policy advocacy often succeeds when there is a collaborative process. Chataway, Joffe, and Mordaunt (2009) recommend thinking beyond results in policy research and engaging stakeholders during all phases of the process. Researchers need to meet with participants, funders, and other stakeholders to clarify issues, try out ideas, and determine what matters most to stakeholders. The research process is an iterative process and can deepen understanding and knowledge. Policy initiatives often may change, which may influence a research project. Therefore, if a reflexive dialogue occurs early in the process, it can help to refine the course of research to make it most relevant to all stakeholders involved (Mayer, 2009).

Communicating research results, including content analysis findings, is most successful when sharing these results strategically. Social workers my present their findings at formal or informal presentations to key stakeholders at breakfast, lunch, or dinner events or in the newspaper. Public workshops with selected invitees from the policy world, as well as experts, academics, and participants in the research, also can be used (Chataway et al., 2009; Reisch, 2009). Which format to use for meetings and how to communicate the results should be carefully weighed before deciding on a choice. The scope of the project—local, national, or international—influences the social work researcher's choice of environmental context and the locations of key stakeholders involved. Social workers also should be clear about the purpose of the meeting and what type of feedback is desired and when a meeting or event is scheduled. The cultural context also may influence the communication of results (Chataway et al., 2009). For example, the language (e.g., formal versus informal) used for certain audiences, especially since research is often of a technical nature, should be carefully considered.

AN ORGANIZATIONAL CASE EXAMPLE

Be the Evidence International (BTEI) is an example of a social work–led research, practice, and advocacy organization that disseminates research for action, including the use of content analysis methods to build awareness and advocacy efforts (BTEI, 2014). Its membership consists of socially and globally conscious researchers, practitioners, educators, policymakers and advocates, and concerned citizens. BTEI's mission is to create awareness of human rights and social justice issues through research, advocacy, and education. Their activities are designed to foster dialogue and action on how health and justice equity can be realized for everyone everywhere, including close to home. It is a non-profit independent scholarly and creative venture designed to disseminate knowledge, values, skills, and system transformation that will help improve the individual, family, and community response to health and justice matters by "any media means necessary." BTEI uses research, education, social innovation, and advocacy as a vehicle to disseminate information in order to raise critical consciousness and the recognition of psychological sociopolitical contexts in which injustices can occur. BTEI's main activities include research and evaluation, program design, policy advocacy, public education and awareness campaigns, and social work and interprofessional education and training. The list of their publications and media outreach information can be found online, at www. betheevidence.org.

CHAPTER SUMMARY

This chapter reviewed the use of content analysis methods for use with public awareness and advocacy at the local and global levels. As reviewed, content analysis can be a powerful method for all stages of the research design, such as conducting a content analysis of the literature to assist in identifying a problem under investigation, conducting a data analysis strategy to analyze primary or secondary data, and developing an action plan. The study findings can help advance the aim of social change and action, which goes directly to the heart and mission of social work. Content analysis findings can serve to enlighten others, including practitioners and policymakers, to take action on social problems and implement solutions.

7

A Case Example Applying Basic and Interpretive Content Analysis to Newly Collected Data

In Chapter 5, on rigor in content analysis studies and reports, we detailed 10 steps for enhancing rigor in content analysis projects that can be applied to the use of either primary or secondary data (Drisko, 1997, 2013b). These steps are (1) starting with a research question of merit and worth, (2) identifying the selected study epistemology, (3) ensuring appropriate research ethics and participant safeguards, (4) stating the research design, (5) clarifying the characteristics of the sample, (6) detailing the data collection methods, (7) detailing coding and data analysis, (8) researcher reflexivity, (9) discussing results, and (10) maintaining the internal consistency of the study.

This chapter provides a case example of how these 10 steps can be applied in a combined basic and interpretive content analysis project. The following content analysis was conducted by the second author, using primary data collected from a mailed survey questionnaires to a sample of 677 persons in prison. The specific study focus was on the narrative responses of a subsample of 201 older adults in prison and their experiences of trauma, stress, and coping in prison. Since this chapter focuses on the content analysis methods, a brief summary of the prior literature justifying this study is not provided here. For a more thorough description of the background of the literature, please see Maschi, Viola, and Koskinen (2015). Directly following a detailed description of the research methods, a summary of results and implications for practice are provided.

STEP ONE: STARTING WITH A RESEARCH QUESTIONS OF MERIT AND WORTH

Step one of a rigorous content analysis project begins with a research question of merit and worth that addresses knowledge and practice gaps based on a review of the literature. The current study is based on a review of the literature in which a dearth of empirical information was found about older adults' experiences of prison, especially as it relates to the trauma and stress of prison and how they coped with these experiences (e.g., Maschi, Viola, Morgen, & Koskinen, 2015). Types of traumatic and stressful life experiences related to mental health symptoms specific to post-traumatic stress disorder are presented in Table 7.1.

Available evidence addressing diverse age groups or people in prison suggests that the social environmental conditions of prison can have a negative physical and mental health effect on people in prison. These negative effects may have a greater impact on older adults because of age-related physical and mental health decline (see, e.g., Maschi, Sutfin, & O'Connor, 2012; Maschi, Viola, & Sun, 2013). Despite the potential adverse effects, the literature suggests potential areas of coping that might foster resilience (e.g., Maschi, Viola, & Morgen, 2014). Existing conceptual frameworks, such as stress process theory, shed light on the how individuals cope in general with trauma and stress (e.g., Krohne, 2002; Lazarus, 1991, 1996,; Pearlin, Schieman, Fazio, & Meersman, 2005). However, these theories have not been applied or tested with older adults in prison. Although there is a growing body of research on stress and coping in prison, many areas of inquiry remained unanswered, especially in regard to the experiences of trauma, stress, and coping among incarcerated older adults. The knowledge gaps identified were as follows: (1) What is the diversity of experience that older people report

Table 7.1. Select Trauma and Stress-Related Disorders in DSM-5 (APA, 2013)

Post-traumatic stress disorder (PTSD)
Criterion
A. The individual was exposed to actual death or threatened death, actual or threatened serious injury, or sexual violence in the form of at least one of the following: (1) direct exposure, (2) witnessing (in person), (3) indirect exposure by learning that a close relative or friend was exposed to trauma (must be violent or accidental for situations of actual or threatened death), or (4) repeated or extreme indirect exposure to an event (e.g., first responders)
B. Intrusion symptoms (one to five symptoms needed): (1) recurrent, involuntary, and intrusive recollections, (2) traumatic nightmares, (3) dissociative symptoms (such as flashbacks), (4) intense prolonged distress after exposure to traumatic reminders, and (5) marked physiological reactivity after exposure to the trauma-related stimuli
C. Persistent avoidance of stimuli associated with the trauma (one of two symptoms needed): (1) trauma-related thought or feelings and (2) trauma-related external reminders (e.g., social interactions, objects, places)
D. Negative changes in cognitions and mood that are associated with the traumatic event (two of seven symptoms needed): (1) inability to recall key features of the traumatic event (e.g., dissociative amnesia), (2) persistent and commonly distorted negative beliefs and expectations about oneself or the world, (3) persistent distorted blame of self and other for causing the trauma or its consequences, (4) persistent negative trauma-related emotions (such as horror, fear, anger, guilt, and shame), (5) markedly diminished interest in (pre-traumatic) significant activities, (6) feeling alienated, detached, or estranged from others, and (7) constricted affect and persistent inability to positive emotions
E. Changes in arousal and reactivity that are associated with the traumatic event (two of six symptoms needed): (1) irritable or aggressive behavior, (2) self-destructive or reckless behavior, (3) hypervigilance, (4) exaggerated startle response, (5) problems in concentration, and (6) sleep disturbance
F. Persistence of symptoms (in criteria of B, C, D, and E) for more than 1 month
G. Significant symptom-related distress or functional impairment
H. Not due to medication, substance misuse, or illness
Other Specified Trauma/Stressor
Adjustment disorder more than 6 months without prolonged duration of trauma/stressor

about the types of trauma and stress experienced in prison? and (2) What do older people report as ways of coping with the prison experience?

This review of the literature provided the justification and rationale to develop research questions of merit and worth with significant implications for developing or improving practice and policy regarding older adults in prisons and other long-term care settings. The purpose of the study was to explore the current experiences of trauma, stress, and coping of adults aged 50 and older in a northeastern U.S. prison system. The research questions were devised by a research team that consisted of experienced academic researchers and one trained doctoral student. The research team developed the following research questions: (1) What do incarcerated older adults report about their current traumatic and stressful life experience in prison? and (2) How do older adults in prison cope with or manage these traumatic or stressful experiences while in prison?

Research on older adults' experiences of trauma, stress, and coping has significant implications for practice and policy, especially in regard to the human rights and social justice issues raised in the treatment of vulnerable populations such as incarcerated people and older adults. More specifically, the findings generated from this study can be used to (1) build public awareness about prison conditions and the treatment of older adults of long-term secure care settings; (2) reveal existing sources of trauma in prison, such as rape and elder abuse; (3) identify sources of resilient coping that are related to maintaining well-being despite the often stressful conditions of confinement; (4) make more informed decisions about the allocation of resources for programs that mediate the potential adverse effects of trauma and stress on health and well-being and facilitate healthier reintegration to communities (post-prison release); and (5) identify areas for practice and policy advocacy, especially since elder abuse and the mistreatment of people in prison are important social work and societal issues.

STEPS TWO THROUGH NINE: METHODS AND IMPLICATIONS

This next section details the decision-making process for steps two through nine in choosing the research methods used to answer the study's research questions. It reviews the study rationale, research design and sampling strategies, sample description, data collection procedures, data sources, data analysis methods, and discussion and implications. It concludes with a brief discussion of the implications for practice, policy, and research.

STEP TWO: IDENTIFYING THE SELECTED STUDY EPISTEMOLOGY

A pragmatist tradition was chosen as the approach to conduct this study. Pragmatism, as it applies to the justification of a claim, rejects the view that all knowledge finally rests on a foundation of objective facts or beliefs (Dewey, 1929). Instead, pragmatists argue that the justification of an argument is a function of a relationship between results and their usefulness (Patton, 2002). That is, scientific findings or concepts should be evaluated according to how effectively they explain or predicts phenomena, rather than how accurately they describe an objective reality. Such views are also vital to Rorty's (1979) "neopragmatism," which disavows ideas of universal truth, objectivity, and epistemological foundationalism. In many ways, pragmatism is closer to a constructivist epistemology than to a positivist one. Yet, like realism, pragmatism supports the utility of concepts and theories even if they cannot currently be empirically tested (e.g., when technology is not available to test a given claim).

The rationale for this choice of pragmatism was as follows: Given the main concepts or constructs (trauma, stress, and coping) under investigation, there is a developed body of literature and available quantitative instruments available, such as the Life Stressors Checklist–Revised (LSC-R; Kimerling, Clum, & Wolfe, 2000) and the Coping Resources Inventory (CRI; Marting & Hammer, 2004). However, at the time of data collection, these measures had not been used with an older adult prison population. Therefore, it was not clear if these measures would adequately capture the diversity of the traumatic and stressful life experiences and coping resources found among this understudied older population and in this this type of setting (prison). In addition, open-ended questions were added to the quantitative measures to determine if there were other experiences that older adults described as traumatic or stressful experiences in prison that were not captured in available quantitative instruments. The pragmatist tradition was selected because it provided support for the use of standardized measures as well as new questions developed by the research team.

Research based on a pragmatist epistemology does not assume that facts and theories are "objective" or unchanging. Research results are located in time, place, and culture, rather than being universal. There are no foundational facts or findings. This would mean researchers adopting a pragmatist epistemology must be careful not to universalize their results. Generalization would require replication in additional settings, with different research participants and in different time periods. Knowledge is, in effect, situational and must be judged on its usefulness in a given setting (Rorty, 1979).

STEP THREE: ENSURING APPROPRIATE RESEARCH ETHICS AND PARTICIPANT SAFEGUARDS

This study was conducted in September 2010 in the New Jersey Department of Corrections. The project was part of the second author's Geriatric Social Work Faculty Scholars Award for a research project on trauma, coping, and well-being among older adults in prison and was funded by the Gerontological Society of America and the John A. Hartford Foundation. The study was jointly approved by the Fordham University Institutional Review Board (IRB) and the New Jersey Department of Corrections Departmental Review Board (DRB). The study was found to meet the standards for conducting research with a special population of older prisoners and that examined sensitive topics such as trauma. The informed consent form used outlined the purpose of the study (to gather information on the past and current experiences of older adults in prison), what was being asked of participants (to complete a 90-minute mailed survey), and core research protections, such as voluntary participation, confidentiality, the risk and benefits of participation, and contact information for the lead researcher and Fordham University IRB. A debriefing statement was included that had contact information for the research team if any participant experienced an adverse response to their taking part in the study.

STEP FOUR: STATING THE STUDY RESEARCH DESIGN

Step four in strategies for enhancing rigor is to state and describe the study research design. The study used a cross-sectional study that was simultaneously descriptive and exploratory. It was descriptive in design because in that it documents the characteristics of a specific sample of older adults and their current experiences of trauma and coping in prison. It was simultaneously exploratory because it provides new information that was not found in prior studies about the current experiences of trauma and coping among older adults in prison (see Chapter 5). The use of a combined descriptive and exploratory research design supports the development of an evidence base using key stakeholders' experiences of trauma and coping in prison among a vulnerable population of older adults. This information can be used to developed evidence-based trauma-informed care, stress management programs, and an advocacy agenda.

STEP FIVE: CLARIFYING THE CHARACTERISTICS OF A SAMPLE

Step five consists of clarifying the characteristics of the sample. To answer this study's research questions about the experiences of trauma and coping among older adults in prison, a sample of older adults housed in the New Jersey Department of Corrections (NJ DOC) in September 2010 was gathered as the sampling frame. The NJ DOC generated a list of names of incarcerated older adults so that invitations and anonymous questionnaires could be mailed to potential participants and return correspondence could be received. The sample consisted of 677 English-speaking incarcerated persons aged 50 and older. Of the approximately 25,000 adults housed in the NJ DOC in January 2010, 7% ($n = 1,750$) were aged 50 and older. The entire population, or census, of 1,750 older adults was invited to participate in the survey. The Dillman, Smyth, and Christian (2009) method for mailed surveys was used to maximize response rates and is outlined next. A total of 677 questionnaires were returned for an approximate 40% response rate. This estimate falls within the higher range of expected mail response rates, which are 20%–40% for prison populations (Hochstetler, Murphy, & Simons, 2004).

Sociodemographic Profile of Study Participants

The sociodemographic and trauma histories of the study sample, with highlights of the participants' personal backgrounds, are found in Table 7.2 and detailed next. The Culturally Responsive Sociodemographic Questionnaire–Prison (CRSQ-P; Maschi, 2010a) was used to gather self-reported background information from participants, which included the following: age, race/ethnicity, gender, marital status,

Table 7.2. Sociodemographic Characteristics of Study Participants (N = 677)

	%	N
Chronological Age		
Young old (aged 50–54)	45.0	288
Middle old (aged 55–64)	44.0	284
Oldest old (aged 65–100)	9.0	60
Race/Ethnicity		
White	35.0	227
African American	45.0	291
Hispanic/Latino	11.0	71
Other	9.0	59
Gender		
Male	96.0	626
Female	4.0	26
Education		
No high school diploma	10.0	65
High school diploma	74.0	481
College degree or above	16.0	101
Religion		
Christian	62.0	335
Islamic/Muslim	13.0	71
Atheist/agnostic	13.0	71
Other	12.0	62
Military History	30.0	196
Marital Status		
Never married	29.0	182
Married	14.0	91
Partnered—not married	11.0	69
Divorced	30.0	187
Separated	7.0	46
Widowed	8.0	50
Other	2.0	11
Family		
One or more children	80.0	504
One or more children <18 years	23.0	129
One or more grandchildren	61.0	365
One or more grandchildren <18 years	56.0	324
Incarcerated family member	48.0	306

Table 7.2. Continued

	%	N
Offense History		
Delinquent offense	36.0	226
Violent offense	64.0	413
Sex offense	25.0	163
Drug offense	46.0	294
Violation of probation	42.0	285
Parole violation	42.0	271
Expected Release Date		
0–1 year	22.0	145
2–5 years	37.0	245
6–10 years	13.0	84
11–50 years	12.0	82
51 years to life	5.0	30
Mental Health or Substance Use History		
Mental health diagnosis	28.0	183
Alcohol problem	25.0	165
Drug problem	44.0	283
Prison mental health treatment	33.0	212
Prison religious participation	72.0	463

educational status, number of children, physical and mental health status, amount of time served, legal history, and expected release date.

Basic descriptive analyses were conducted using SPSS 20.0. As indicated in Table 7.2, on average, participants were 61 years old (SD = 5.43), although the group was evenly distributed between young old (50–54; 45%) and middle old (55–64; 44%). The majority of participants were either African American (45%) or white (35%) and male (96%). Approximately 9 out of 10 (90%) participants had received at least their high school diploma. As for self-reported religious affiliation, 62% identified as Christian. Approximately 30% reported a history of being in the military. One-quarter (25%) of participants reported currently being married or partnered. Most participants reported having children (80%) and grandchildren (61%). One-half of participants (48%) reported having at least one other incarcerated family member. Sixty-four percent of participants reported having a violent offense history and 5% had been sentenced to life in prison. The length of prison term varied from 4 months to 42 years served; the average was 13 years served. Twenty-two percent reported eligibility for parole within 1 year and 26% reported they were eligible in 2 to 5 years. Twenty-eight percent of participants reported a history of mental health problems; another quarter reported a history of alcohol use and 44% reported a history of drug use. Participants reported a lower frequency of participation in mental health treatment (33%) than in religious services (72%).

As shown in Table 7.3, participants reported chronic health problems, such as arthritis (17%), hypertension, (15%), heart problems or cardiovascular disease (10%), diabetes (10%), HIV/AIDS (4%), and cancer (3%). Additional health issues that suggest disability included vision problems (20%), problems pertaining to the back or neck (20%), walking difficulties (11%), lung and breathing issues (10%), and hearing impairment (5%). Each of these issues may pose difficulties for individuals endeavoring to keep up with the pace of the prison regimen or to

Table 7.3. Descriptive Statistics for Physical and Mental Health Issues ($N = 677$)

	%	N
Physical Health		
Arthritis/rheumatism	17.0	112
Hypertension	15.0	101
Walking problem	11.0	72
Fractures, bone/joint injury	11.0	71
Heart problem	10.0	65
Diabetes	10.0	63
Stroke	2.0	10
HIV/AIDS	4.0	28
Cancer	3.0	16
Eye/vision problem	20.0	132
Back or neck problem	20.0	130
Lung/breathing problem	10.0	63
Hearing problem	5.0	33
Other impairment	8.0	53
Mental Health (Most Serious Diagnosis)		
Depression	8.0	56
Bipolar disorder	5.0	30
Post-traumatic stress disorder	3.0	18
Schizophrenia or schizoaffective disorder	2.0	15
Other	4.0	26

participate in programs or activities that could foster resilience. Two out of three participants reported a history of some type of serious mental illness, such as major depression (8%) or bipolar disorder (5%).

Although this study focused on current trauma and stress in prison, it is important to note that participants also reported earlier life experiences of trauma and stress prior to their current prison sentence. The majority reported having experienced some type of earlier life trauma, grief, loss, or separation experience, such as being a victim of violence (24%), a witness to violence (48%), or in combat or war (15%). Many participants also reported experiencing other earlier life stressors, such as the unexpected or expected death of a loved one (70%), financial stress (53%), family caregiving stress (25%), prior jail or prison term (54%), or having an incarcerated family member (60%). Some of these experiences, such as witnessing violence, may have been a result of committing a crime, but this was not verifiable in the quantitative data findings. See Maschi and colleagues' studies (Maschi, Sutfin, & O'Connor, 2012; Maschi, Viola, & Morgen, 2014; Maschi, Viola, & Sun, 2013) for more details on cumulative trauma experiences of this population.

STEP SIX: DETAILING THE DATA COLLECTION METHODS

In this study, the Dillman et al. (2009) four-step method for self-administered mailed surveys was used to gather data from a sample of older adults in prison. Specifically, potential participants received (1) a letter of invitation; (2) a packet with a cover letter, consent form, survey, and a self-addressed electronically stamped envelope (SASE) 7 days later; and (3) two thank you cards and reminders sent 7 days apart that included an enclosed self-addressed envelope for participants to request a survey replacement.

Trauma, Stress, and Coping

The survey questionnaire consisted of quantitative and qualitative data sources, which included quantitative survey instruments and open-ended questions to gather specific information from the sample of incarcerated older adults about their personal experiences of trauma, stress, and coping in prison. The specific data on trauma, stress, and coping were gathered from participants' responses on the Life Stressors Checklist-Revised (LSC-R; Wolfe, Kimerling, Brown, Chrestman, & Levin, 1996) and the Prison Stress and Coping Scale–Short (PSCS-S, Maschi, 2010b). The LSC-R is a 31-item scale that measures frequencies of objective occurrences of lifetime and current traumatic events. It also accounts for stressful life events, such as losing a loved one, health problems, divorce, financial problems, and institutional stress and abuse. Past-year subjective distress is measured by the extent to which participants report how much they were affected (not at all to extremely affected) by each event in the past year. The LSC-R has good psychometric properties, including use with diverse age groups and criminal justice populations (e.g., Kimerling et al., 2000; Wolfe & Kimerling, 1997). Researchers have reported that the LSC-R demonstrates good criterion-related validity among criminal justice populations, including test–retest Kappas of .70 (McHugo et al., 2005).

For the purposes of this study, only one question addressed the experience of trauma and stress in prison: "Have you ever experienced stress or abuse in prison?" Participants could respond as to whether or not these experiences occurred (yes or no). They then gave their subjective response (feeling horror or threatened at the time; yes or no) and conveyed how much the experience affected them in the past year (not at all to extremely affected). The Life Stressors Checklist-Revised (LSC-R) was completed by the entire sample ($N = 677$). About 201 participants also provided a written response to the open-ended portion of the question (if yes, what was the event), which provided qualitative data.

The PSCS-S (Maschi, 2010b) also was used to gather data about the sample of older adults' experiences of trauma, stress, and coping in prison. The PSCS-S consists of two open-ended questions: "What are the types of things that caused you stress while in prison in the past month?" and "What kind of things did you do in the past month, if anything at all, to help with your stress?"

STEP SEVEN: DETAILING CODING AND DATA ANALYSIS

For the purposes of this study, NVivo 9.0 (2010) was used to generate univariate descriptive analysis to calculate frequencies and percentages for one item from the LSC-R in which participants reported whether they experienced prison-related stress and abuse (yes or no) and a one item about if participants indicated they used one or more strategies to cope with prison stress (yes/no). The results of these descriptive analyses on coping is illustrated in Table 7.4 (see column one).

Table 7.4. Sources of Coping Resources and Activities (N = 201)

Coping Domains	Description	Sample Quotes
Root (12%, n = 24)	Basic needs/ foundation: Food, clothing, safety, grounded in love and family	"I try to be secure in myself," "I feel safer at the minimum-security prison compared to a maximum one."
Physical (33%, n = 66)	Exercise (yard, run/walk, sports), medication	"I became a jogger and sprinter at 56 years old. I run 5 miles per day and sprint 105 yard sprints every other day."
Cognitive (35%, n = 70)	Find peace within, think positive, making healthy choices, doing puzzles, read	"I try to think positive and try to meditate and read a great deal to take my mind off worries."
Emotional (23%, n = 46)	Supportive emotional counseling, anger and stress management, music (listening)	"I participate every Monday in group therapy. Cage Your Rage program 10 weeks"
Social (54%, n = 108))	Interaction with family, friends, or peers in prison, program participation	"I keep in touch with family members."
Spiritual (37%, n = 34)	Church, God, prayer, service to others	"Pray to God and go to church regularly here."
Participatory (13%, n = 26)	Leadership, taking classes or vocational training for personal advancement, teaching, leading a book club, advocacy	"I lead a bereavement group for other inmates." "I am a paralegal and seek justice for people in prison."
Multidimensional (7%, n = 14)	Art-making, music-making, yoga	"I do yoga, doctor, I do yoga."

A combination of basic and interpretive content analysis methods were used to analyze the data responses to the open-ended questions about trauma, stress, and coping in prison. These different content analysis approaches are outlined in Chapters 1–4 of this text and specifically draw on content analysis strategies from Krippendorff (2004), Neuendorf (2002), and Tutty and colleagues (1996).

As described throughout this text, content analysis is a systematic procedure used to code and analyze qualitative data, such as qualitative survey data, and a combination of deductive and inductive approaches can be used (Bernard & Ryan, 2010; Krippendorff, 2013). Therefore, a combination of basic and interpretive content analysis methods were used to analyzed the data in this study and are detailed next.

Trauma and Stress

The trauma and stress data were analyzed using both basic and interpretive content analysis strategies using an inductive approach. For the inductive analysis strategies to analyze trauma and stress, Tutty, Rothery, and Grinnell's (1996) four-step qualitative data analysis strategies were used. This qualitative data analysis method is similar to constant comparative methods found in grounded theory (Strauss & Corbin, 1998). For the inductive analysis, step one involved identifying "meaning units" (or in vivo codes) from the data. For example, the assignment of meaning units included assigning codes to reflect the types of trauma and stress in prison that were identified by participants. In step two, second-level coding and first-level meaning units were sorted and placed in their emergent categories (e.g., interpersonal, social, cultural, structural, and internalized). Meaning unit codes were arranged by clustering similar codes into a category or theme and separating dissimilar codes to create distinct categories. A list of the codes generated can be found in Figure 7.1. Prison trauma and stress were coded and classified at the following levels: cultural, structural, social, interpersonal, and internalized. The categories were then analyzed for themes and patterns or the relationship between them. In step three, the categories were examined for meaning and interpretation. In step four, a conceptually clustered diagram was constructed to illustrate the patterns and themes found in the data (see Figure 7.1) (Miles & Huberman, 1994).

Once the inductive data were coded, a basic content analysis was conducted to determine the frequency counts of the number of participants

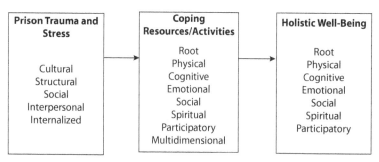

Figure 7.1. A conceptual model of prison trauma and stress, coping resources/ activities, and holistic well-being among older adults in prison. As the study findings suggest, older people in prison reported tapping into coping resources (i.e., root, physical, cognitive, emotional, social, spiritual, and participatory or leadership activities) to deal with prison trauma and stress at the cultural, structural, social, interpersonal, and internalized levels. Those participants who reported engaging in coping activities also reported feeling a subjective or internal sense of well-being associated with these activities. These domains of holistic well-being include root (e.g., sense of safety and security), physical, cognitive, emotional, social, spiritual, and participatory (e.g., feeling empowered and having a sense of purpose).

(n = 201) who reported experiencing one or more of these traumatic and/or stressful experiences. These results appear as percentages in the findings section for each of the types of prison trauma and stress that older adults reported experiencing in prison.

Coping

In this study we also used a deductive approach and basic content analysis strategies to conduct frequency counts of already identified a priori or preexisting categories of coping resources (i.e., physical, cognitive, emotional, social, and spiritual coping) to extract the data and conduct frequency counts of the data (Krippendorff, 2004). Counts of textual variables were then calculated to identify frequencies and percentages using the descriptive statistics function of NVivo 9.0. Given that the CRI did not capture all of the types of coping resources that older people in prison reported using, a category of "other" was used. Interpretive qualitative analysis techniques were used to classify the textual data classified as "other" than the five a priori categories of coping resources and this 'other' data were analyzed inductively for latent content. See Table 7.4 and Figure 7.1 for a list of a priori codes and findings (i.e., physical, cognitive, emotional, social, and spiritual coping) and interpretive codes (i.e., root, participatory, and multidimensional).

Inter-Coder Reliability

For all analyses, two coders were used until 95% to 100% of agreement was obtained. To enhance trustworthiness, strategies for rigor were used that included an audit trail and peer debriefing. The use of an audit trail resulted in a report detailing the decision-making for each step taken in coding, data analysis, and interpretation. The research team maintained detailed analytic and self-reflective memos to record their process and progress. These strategies increased the dependability of the findings because a systematic approach to documentation was used. It also ensured confirmability since the findings were firmly linked to the data and corroborated in peer debriefing sessions.

STEP EIGHT: RESEARCHER REFLEXIVITY

The lead researcher and members of the research team engaged in critical self-reflection and peer debriefing during research process and in particular the data analysis process. All three team members included in their memos an ongoing assessment of their positionality based on age, race, ethnicity, gender, class, professional experience, and trauma and criminal legal histories. Any potential biases that may have existed about participants were noted, especially those regarding age and persons with criminal justice histories, particularly of violent offenses. In peer debriefing sessions, group discussion addressed potential blind spots around recognizing the source of trauma and stress identified by incarcerated participants, such as separation from family. There was a biased tendency among some members of the research team to assume that society discounts family separation as a legitimate source of trauma and stress that transcends the individual responsibility for criminal behavior that sentenced them to prison.

STEP NINE: DISCUSSING RESULTS

As described in Chapter 5, step nine (discussing results) often provides abductive interpretations based on the study results. This next section summarizes and describes the major findings, the abductively inferred implications for practice and policy, research limitations, and future research directions.

Trauma, Stress, and Coping in Prison

As outlined earlier, for the purpose of this study, the data for trauma and stress in prison were drawn from the following LSC-R items: "Have you ever experienced abuse or other stress while in prison (yes or no)?" and "If yes, what was the event?" When participants were asked if they had experienced trauma and stress in prison, more than half (53%) of the entire sample (n = 677) reported experiencing current abuse and stress in prison, and among those, 86% felt moderately to extremely affected by it in the past year. As described earlier, the qualitative content analysis focused on the current experiences of prison trauma and stress among older adults in prison as expressed in their responses to the open-ended question to describe their experience of abuse and stress in prison.

We also relied on qualitative data from open-ended questions on two items on the PSCS-S regarding trauma, stress, and coping. The first question, "What are the types of things that caused you stress while in prison in the past month?" provided additional qualitative data on participants' experience of trauma and stress. The second question, "What kind of things did you do in the past month, if anything at all, to help with your stress?" provided information on how participants reported coping with prison. A subsample of 201 participants provided a first-hand, detailed description of current experiences of prison trauma, stress, and coping (during the past month) that influenced their sense of safety and feelings of well-being. A conceptual model of the collective study findings can be found in Figure 7.1.

Trauma and Stress: Findings

The most prominent descriptions of current prison trauma and stress were categorized as either external—for example, interpersonal, social, cultural, and structural, trauma and stress—or internal—for example, internalized negative self-talk. Identified coping practices or resources that participants reported engaging in to cope with trauma and stress of incarceration that helped improve their sense of well-being were categorized as root (basic needs), physical, cognitive, emotional, social, spiritual, participatory, and multidimensional.

Interpersonal Trauma and Stress
Based on the narratives, we describe *interpersonal* trauma and oppression as one-on-one interpersonal abuse, neglect, bullying, or harassment. About one-third of participants reported experiencing interpersonal oppression from correctional or medical staff or other inmates which included demeaning attitudes and unjust actions. Of the 31% of participants who reported interpersonal trauma, 43% reported that these experiences occurred with staff and 18% with other incarcerated persons, and 15% reported experiencing oppressive attitudes, beliefs, and practices in their interactions with both staff and other incarcerated persons.

The firsthand accounts of participants shed light on the harsh reality of the life of an incarcerated older adult, who may be a victim of or witness minor to severe trauma, abuse, and violence. Some participants described others' condescending attitudes, "bias from guards/security officers," and "harassment from officers." Others reported "being picked on for petty things," "constant shakedowns," and "canceled recreation." Participants reported a high level of stress living with the reality that "you could be set up by an officer at any given time, just because they don't like you," or "being punished for other people's actions," or "being accused of things you didn't do and your job taken away." Significant distress was associated with a "male guard feeling on my body." One participant reported witnessing "corrections officers stomping inmates into comas."

Participants also shared feelings of distress associated with interactions with other incarcerated people. Some examples of this source of peer-to-peer stress included "ignorance of inmates," "immature inmates, arguments," "being among fellow prisoners who have no honor, little integrity, and who revel in depravity (just like the guards)," "bias from gang members," "aggression from other inmates," "getting into fights with other inmates," and "being robbed." One older participant feared for his safety and said, "I am 72 years old and I am afraid of getting raped again."

Social Trauma and Stress

Almost half (45%) of the participants reported *social* trauma and stress, predominantly separation from family and the community. One man said, "I am confined like an animal and kept away from family." Others reported feeling stressed about "being here away from my family and not having freedoms," "being transferred to a prison where my loved ones couldn't visit because of the distance," or lack of contact: "I cannot contact family, I think about my children, grandkids, children in DYFS." One respondent noted: "It is hard for me 'cause my son's mother ain't with me now. She's on my mind and I think about my kids and new granddaughter." Poor mail delivery, lack of phones, and families often stressed due to lack of resources or other members incarcerated were common complaints.

Cultural Trauma and Stress

About 15% reported that *cultural* or societal attitudes toward incarcerated people that were reenacted by staff and other incarcerated people caused them stress. In particular, the prison culture fosters the "subhuman status of being labeled prisoners" conveyed by prison staff and society in general. The stigma of incarceration and the loss of identity are communicated by responses such as "you're identified as a number, and not as a human being," and "as long as you're in khaki, you are considered non-human." One participant noted, "You can't get an answer from Department of Corrections or from social workers" and "corrections officers disrespect inmates and beat them up."

Structural Trauma and Stress

Roughly one out of three participants (29%) reported *structural* trauma and stress. Almost two-thirds of these participants reported that the sources of trauma and stress were attributed to laws, policies, and institutional regulations. Several participants reported that staff often created and enforced their own informal rules while failing to enforce existing institutional policies, such as responding to prison abuse. One participant made the following observation about correctional officers: "They seem to lack a 'higher power' to address prison abuse and neglect."

Participants described feelings of powerlessness and stress as well, particularly in response to unjust laws and policies and lack of family support as they attempted to navigate the legal process. One participant noted, "my family is not downloading the files from the Internet to help me with my appeal."

One-third of participants reported trauma and stress related to poor nutrition and inadequate healthcare within the prison. One respondent wrote, "food nutrition poor; variety—poor; balance—none; lack of use of utilities; water—no water to drink for 2 days; food, meat not cooked; not getting out to yard enough," and "everyone chain smokes around me all the time." Other responses often referred to medical neglect; these included the following: "there is indifference to my need for medical care;" "medical department ignoring medical complaints;" "there's a failure of medical personnel, malpractice, a failure to treat, negligence, abuse, denial of vital medication, heart meds;" "a failure to follow specialists' recommendations for treatment of hypertension and pain;" "there's mismanagement of prison and neglect of serious health issues;" "I have constant back pain, scoliosis, lumbar/thoracic spine," and "I get no medical attention when my tooth throbs." Female participants shared that healthcare services were inadequate for the special needs of older women. One participant lamented, "I would not wish this place on my worst enemy."

Administration and staff's abusive and neglectful practices included extreme forms of confinement and isolation: "prison officers confine inmates in two cages 15–20 minutes for all three meals 7 days a week;" "I've been locked up in a room for 23 hours a day for the past 4 months without an explanation from administration;" "locked up in a cell 22 hours a day and not enough recreation time;" "there's a lack of programs to keep the mind active;" and "there are searches where property becomes destroyed or stolen." Others described stress as a result of living with "constant noise" and cells that are "constantly lit up" and feelings of despondency associated with "having to wait 2 to 4 years to participate in a prison program." One older participant noted age biases with the structure of prison: "Prisons are designed for young people. Us older folks find it hard to get a job or education here."

Internalized: "Negative Self-Talk"
In response to the trauma and stress of confinement, some participants reported adverse psychological and emotional responses to the trauma and stress of incarceration. These responses were identified as *negative*

self-talk in which participants have internal narratives that cause them psychological and emotional distress. Negative thoughts or emotions included anxiety, fear, worry, depression, insecurity, feelings of lone-liness and defeat, hopelessness, apathy, grief, anger, guilt, and shame. Some participants reported feeling anxiety about their personal health and safety, being separated from children and other family members, the physical and emotional heath of their children, and the uncertainty of their future. Several participants who were close to being released from prison described their bleak options for future employment and economic earning power. Participants shared: "I worry about when I get out—getting kids a place to live;" "keeping a job to make ends meet;" "I am scared about job opportunities upon my release, rebuilding rela-tionships with my children" and "not being able to support them." One respondent wrote: "I believe the intent is for us to die in here."

Some participants described feeling tormented as they grappled with the implications of their crime. One participant described fearing that "others will learn the details of my crime." Other participants thought about how their crime affected others. They shared, "I constantly relive the decision which put me back in prison and caused me to lose every-thing, my wife, kids, car, all money, and possessions." "I feel guilt—my family was harmed by my actions . . . how will I face my family?"

Coping Resources

The conceptual matrix for coping resources can be found in Table 7.4. As illustrated in Table 7.4, despite the trauma and stress of incarceration, many participants reported adaptive responses to managing the prison experience and overall well-being, such as having a positive outlook. In contrast to pharmaceutical interventions, these self-care activities offer low-cost solutions to fostering health and well-being, including for older people in prison. Our content analysis results revealed that the variety of coping resources or practices reported by older adults in prison were categorized as root (foundational needs), physical, cogni-tive, emotional, social, spiritual, participatory, and multidimensional. As shown in Table 7.4, the majority of participants (54%) relied on social coping strategies to deal with the stressors of confinement, followed by spiritual (37%), cognitive (35%), and physical (33%). Almost two-thirds (63%) of participants reported participating in two activities of coping; nearly one-quarter (23%) indicated that they participated in as many as nine activities. Some individuals indicated that they participated in no activities by choice, which could be related to their physical health, or because there were no activities available to them. A promising finding is the effective use of participatory or empowerment practices in which participants are able to demonstrate leadership and engage in personal advancement or advocacy (see Table 7.4). For example, one participant noted, "I have been facilitating a grief bereavement program once a week for 12 years and another group 3 times a year for the past 17 years." These coping resources or practices have promise for fostering resilience and well-being among older people, despite the traumatic and stressful conditions of confinement.

STEP TEN: MAINTAINING THE INTERNAL CONSISTENCY OF THE STUDY

This section outlines how step nine (maintaining internal consistency of the study) was applied to the summary and discussion of the abductive inferences made from the findings for practice, policy, and research. In summary, this study described and explored the experiences of trauma, stress, and coping among a sample of older adults in the New Jersey state prison population. Participants identified the sources of prison trauma and stress as social (45%), interpersonal (31%), cultural (15%), and structural (29%). Almost half of the participants responded with specificity that separation from family and community was a source of trauma and stress; references to concerns for family were categorized as interpersonal or institutional (e.g., being denied phone privileges; stigma of incarceration; not being able to support children) and suggest that the vulnerability and conflict over this separation is pervasive. This finding is not surprising considering that most participants are parents (80%) and/or grandparents (61%) and at the time of the survey still had more than 2 years of prison time remaining (62%). It is important to note that although age discrimination may have been a factor in the treatment of older people in prison, participants did not always identify age as an explicit source of prison trauma and stress.

Based on these findings, abjductive inferences exist for practice and policy implications. The findings suggest that reducing trauma and stress of prison and increasing coping capacities among older adults in prison should involve a multifaceted strategy to improve the health and well-being of older adults in prison. These strategies may include establishing a more supportive, safer, and more secure prison environment, and providing linkages to family and better access to health, social, and legal and victims' services. Specific programs that might enhance the different domains of coping might include stress management, peer leadership opportunities, family and volunteer prison visiting and service programs, pen pal programs, intergenerational caregiver support services and televisiting services, literacy and exercise programs, chronic illness healthcare clinics, care transitions, and community reintegration programs.

Based on these findings, abductive inferences for policy and policy advocacy can be made. The study found that participants reported prison experiences such as sexual and physical victimization, witnessing violence and abuse, medical neglect, and denial of food and access to work and rehabilitation services. Older adults often described these experiences of trauma and stress as exacerbating their physical and mental health. These experiences can be classified as violations of human rights (ACLU, 2012; HRW, 2012). For example, one older adults described "being 72 and being raped again in prison." Sexual victimization in prison is illegal (see Prison Rape Elimination Act [PREA]) and also can be categorized as elder abuse, also illegal. The World Health Organization (2012) defines elder abuse as a "a single or repeated act, or lack of appropriate action, occurring within any relationship where there is an expectation of trust which causes harm or distress to an older person" (p. 1). Elder abuse may take many forms and consists of physical, sexual, psychological, emotional, or financial exploitation, and intentional or unintentional neglect, including medical neglect (UN, 2012). Many of the participants' descriptions can be classified as a type of elder abuse. Human rights and social protections also can be classified as a type of "cruel and unusual punishment" that could support advocacy efforts to extend elder abuse protections to older adults in prison.

Study Limitations

This research study has limitations that warrant discussion. The qualitative data were collection from a group of incarcerated adults aged 50 and older from one northeastern prison system and cannot be transferable to other geographic locations in the United States or abroad. Although the data from over 201 participants were analyzed to the point of saturation, it is quite possible that not all accounts of trauma and stress in prison among older adults were captured in this study. Since this qualitative study focused specifically on prison trauma, stress, and coping experiences, questions did not fully explore how participants created meaning from their past and current experiences. This study also did not compare younger with older prisoners so it cannot be fully determined whether older prisoners have qualitatively different experiences due to the aging process, nor the extent to which reported experiences and responses may be applicable to other age groups. Additionally, age discrimination may have been a factor in the treatment of older people in prison but not identified as such by participants and thus not reported. Since this study is a cross-sectional examination, we cannot prove that the participants' use of coping activities actually improves health and well-being beyond the participants' subjective reporting that it does.

Future Directions for Research

Despite these limitations, this study lays a foundation for future research on trauma, stress, and coping experiences among older adults, especially those in secure care settings such as prisons. Future research should include mixed-methods designs and should examine how past and current life events and coping experiences shape health, well-being, and criminogenic thinking and behavior over time. Additionally, teasing out the role of age differences and age discrimination is an important area to pursue using age cohorts and quantitative and qualitative measures that assess age and other forms of discrimination and can assess for age-related differences in trauma and stress experiences. Additionally, future research should explore interventions that incorporate multi-modal coping resources (e.g., root, physical, cognitive, emotional, social, spiritual, and participatory) that can be developed and tested for their impact on trauma and stress symptomatology among older adults in prison. Given the importance of medical neglect and social trauma in the current findings, future research should more fully explore these sources of trauma and stress as a form of elder abuse, mistreatment, and neglect, including social exclusion and isolation.

CHAPTER SUMMARY

This chapter applied the 10 steps for achieving rigor in content analysis approaches. It used qualitative data collected from a sample of 677 and a subsample of 201 incarcerated older adults about their experiences of trauma, stress, and coping in prison. The following 10 steps were applied: (1) starting with a research question of merit and worth, (2) identifying the selected study epistemology, (3) ensuring appropriate research ethics and participant safeguards, (4) stating the research design, (5) clarifying the characteristics of the sample, (6) detailing the data collection methods, (7) detailing coding and data analysis, (8) researcher reflexivity, (9) discussing results, and (10) maintaining internal consistency of the study. Social work researchers can use these steps to guide them in designing content analysis studies that incorporate the use of primary or secondary data. Abductive inferences can be made using a critical lens to draw action steps for practice and policy reform.

References

Ahuvia, A. (2001). Traditional, interpretive, and reception based content analyses: Improving the ability of content analysis to address issues of pragmatic and theoretical concern. *Social Indicators Research*, *54*(2), 139–172.

Allport, G. (1942). *The use of personal documents in psychological science*. New York: Social Science Research Council.

Allport, G. (1965). *Letters from Jenny*. New York: Harcourt, Brace and World.

Altheide, D. (1987). Ethnographic content analysis. *Qualitative Sociology*, *10*, 65–77.

Altheide, D., & Schneider, C. (2013). *Qualitative media analysis*. Thousand Oaks, CA: Sage.

American Civil Liberties Union [ACLU]. (2012). *The mass incarceration of the elderly*. Retrieved from www.aclu.org/files/assets/elderlyprisonreport_20120613_1.pdf

American Psychiatric Association [APA]. (2013). *Diagnostic and statistical manual of mental disorders* (5th ed.). Washington, DC: Author.

Anastas, J. (1999). *Research design for social work and the human services* (2nd ed.). New York: Columbia University Press.

Aristotle. (2000). *The rhetoric and the poetics of Aristotle* (Rev. ed.). New York: MacMillan (Original work published 350 BCE).

Austin, D. (2003). The history of social work research. In R. L. Edwards (Ed.-in-Chief), *Encyclopedia of social work* (19th ed., Vol. 1, pp. 81–94). Washington, DC: NASW Press.

Bandura, A. (2001). Social cognitive theory: An agentic perspective. *Annual Review of Psychology, 52*, 1–26.

Barnes, G. (2008). Perspectives of African-American women on infant mortality. *Social Work in Health Care, 47*(3), 292–305.

Bartlett, J. (1969). *A complete concordance to Shakespeare*. New York: Palgrave/Macmillan.

Bartlett, M., Littlewort, G., Frank, M., & Lee, K. (2014). Automatic decoding of facial movements reveals deceptive pain expressions. *Current Biology, 24*(7), 738–743.

Bauer, J., Qualmann, J., Stadtmüller, G., & Bauer, H. (1998). Lebenslaufuntersuchungen bei Alzheimer-Patienten: Qualitative Inhaltsanalyse prämorbider Entwicklungsprozesse. In A. Kruse (Ed.), Psychosoziale Gerontologie. Band 2: Intervention (pp. 251–274). Göttingen, Germany: Hogrefe.

Baxter, L. (1991). Content analysis. In B. Montgomery & S. Duck (Eds.), *Studying interpersonal interaction* (pp. 239–254). New York: Guilford Press.

Benner, P. (1994). The tradition and skill of interpretive phenomenology in studying health, llness, and caring practices. In P. Benner (Ed.), *Interpretive phenomenology: embodiment, caring, and ethics in health and illness* (pp. 99–127). Thousand Oaks, CA: Sage.

Berelson, B. (1952). *Content analysis in communication research*. Glencoe, IL: The Free Press.

Berg, B. (1995). *Qualitative research methods for the social sciences* (2nd ed.). Needham Heights, MA: Allyn & Bacon.

Berg, B. (2001). *Qualitative research methods for the social sciences* (4th ed.). Boston: Allyn & Bacon.

Berg, B. (2008). *Qualitative research methods for the social sciences* (7th ed). Boston: Allyn & Bacon.

Berger, A. (1991). *Media research techniques*. Newbury Park, CA: Sage.

Bernard, H., & Ryan, G. (2010) *Analyzing qualitative data: Systematic approaches*. Thousand Oaks, CA: Sage.

Be the Evidence International [BTEI] (2014). *Be the evidence international*. Retrieved from www.betheevidence.org

Bloom, M. (1980). A working definition of primary prevention related to social concerns. *Journal of Prevention, 1*(1), 15–23.

Boyatzis, R. (1998). *Transforming qualitative information: Thematic analysis and code development*. Thousand Oaks, CA: Sage.

Braun, V., & Clarke, V. (2006). Using thematic analysis in psychology. *Qualitative Research in Psychology, 3*(2), 89–99.

Braun, V., & Clarke, V. (2013). *Successful qualitative research: A guide for beginners*. Thousand Oaks, CA: Sage.

Bulmer, M. (1979). Concepts in the analysis of qualitative data. *The Sociological Review, 27*(4), 651–677.

Campbell, C., & Murphy, A. (1980). *Things we said today: The complete concordance of the Beatles' song lyrics.* Ypsilanti, MI: Pierian Press.

Carpenter, D. (2007). Phenomenology as method. In H. Streubert & D. Carpenter (Eds.), *Qualitative research in nursing: Advancing the humanistic imperative* (pp. 75–99). Philadelphia, PA: Lippincott.

Centre for Civil Society. (2003). *An activist's guide to research and advocacy.* Retrieved from www.csrsc.org.za/Documents%5Cactivism%20and%20research%20manual.pdf

Chan, C., Ho, A., Leung, P., Chochinov, H., Neimeyer, R., Pang, S., & Tse, D. (2012). The blessings and the curses of filial piety on dignity at the end of life: Lived experience of Hong Kong Chinese adult children caregivers. *Journal of Ethnic & Cultural Diversity in Social Work, 21*(4), 277–296.

Chataway, J., Joffe, A., & Mordaunt, J. (2009). Communicating results. In A. Thomas & G. Mohan (Eds.), *Research skills for policy and development: How to find out fast* (pp. 95–110). Thousand Oaks, CA: Sage Publications.

Cohen, D., & Crabtree, B. (2008). Evaluative criteria for qualitative research in health care: Controversies and recommendations. *Annals of Family Medicine, 6*(4), 331–339.

Crabtree, B., & Miller, W. (Eds.). (1999). *Doing qualitative research* (2nd ed.). Thousand Oaks, CA: Sage.

Creswell, J. (2007). *Qualitative inquiry and research design: Choosing among five approaches.* Thousand Oaks, CA: Sage Publications.

Creswell, J. (2011). Controversies in mixed methods research. In N. Denzin & Y. Lincoln, (Eds.), *Handbook of qualitative research* (4th ed., pp. 269–283). Thousand Oaks, CA: Sage.

Creswell, J., & Plano Clark, (2010). *Designing and conducting mixed methods research.* Thousand Oaks, CA: Sage.

Cronbach, L. (1951). Coefficient alpha and the internal structure of tests. *Psychometrika, 16,* 297–333.

Cronbach, L. (2004). *My current thoughts on coefficient alpha and successor procedures.* (Center for Evaluation Studies Report 643). Retrieved from www.cse.ucla.edu/products/reports/r643.pdf

Cronbach, L. & Meehl, P. (1955). Construct validity in psychological tests. *Psychological Bulletin, 52,* 281–302.

Dalrymple, J., & Boylan, J. (2013). *Effective advocacy in social work.* Thousand Oaks, CA: Sage Publications.

Dattalo, P. (2008). *Determining sample size: Balancing power, precision, and practicality.* New York: Oxford University Press.

Denzin, N. (1970). *The research act: A theoretical introduction to sociological methods.* Chicago: Aldine.

Denzin, N., & Lincoln, Y. (2005). Introduction: The discipline and practice of qualitative research. In N. Denzin & Y. Lincoln (Eds.), *The handbook of qualitative research* (3rd ed., pp. 1–32). Thousand Oaks, CA: Sage.

de Sola Pool, I. (1960). Content analysis for intelligence purposes. *World Politics, 12*(3), 478–485.

Dewey, J. (1929). *Experience and nature.* New York: Dover.

Dillman, D., Smyth, J., & Christian, L. (2009). *Internet, mail, and mixed-mode surveys: The tailored design method* (3rd ed.). Hoboken, NJ: John Wiley and Sons.

Dollard, J., & Mowrer, O. (1947). A method of measuring tension in written documents. *Journal of Abnormal & Social Psychology, 42*, 3–32.

Dovring, K. (1954-55). Quantitative semantics in 18th century Sweden. *Public Opinion Quarterly, 18*(4), 389–394.

Drisko, J. (1997). Strengthening qualitative studies and reports: Standards to enhance academic integrity. *Journal of Social Work Education, 33*, 187–197.

Drisko, J. (2003, January 17). Improving sampling strategies and terminology in qualitative research. Paper presented at the Society for Social Work and Research Annual Meeting, Washington, DC.

Drisko, J. (2008). How is qualitative research taught at the master's level? *Journal of Social Work Education, 44*(1), 85–101.

Drisko, J. (2013a). Constructivist research in social work. In R. Fortune, W. Reid, & R. Miller (Eds.), *Qualitative research in social work* (2nd ed., pp. 81–106). New York: Columbia University Press.

Drisko, J. (2013b). Standards for qualitative studies and reports. In R. Fortune, W. Reid, & R. Miller (Eds.), *Qualitative research in social work* (2nd ed., pp. 3–34). New York: Columbia University Press.

Eco, U. (1976). *A theory of semiotics.* Bloomington: Indiana University Press.

Elo, S. Kääriäinen, M., Kanste, O., Pölkki, T., Utriainen, K., & Kyngäs, H. (2014). Qualitative content analysis: A focus on trustworthiness. *Sage Open* (online journal). doi: 10.1177/2158244014522633. Retrieved from http://sgo.sagepub.com/content/4/1/2158244014522633

Engel, R., & Schutt, R. (2013). *The practice of research in social work* (3rd ed.) Thousand Oaks, CA: Sage Publications.

Eysenbach, G., & Till, J. (2001). Ethical issues in qualitative research on internet communities. *British Medical Journal, 323*, 1103–1105. Retrieved from http://bmj.bmjjournals.com/cgi/content/full/323/7321/1103

Finn, J., & Dillon, C. (2007). Using personal ads and online self-help groups to teach content analysis in a research methods course. *Journal of Teaching in Social Work, 27*, 155–164.

Finkelhor, D., Cross, T.P., & Cantor, E. (2005). *How the justice system responds to juvenile victims: A comprehensive model*. Washington, DC: Office of Juvenile Justice and Delinquency Prevention.

Finlay, L. (2002). Negotiating the swamp: The opportunity and challenge of reflexivity in research practice. *Qualitative Research, 2*(2), 209–230.

Fisher, D., Hill, D., Grube, J., & Gruber E. (2007). Gay, lesbian, and bisexual content on television: A quantitative analysis across two seasons. *Journal of Homosexuality, 52*(3-4), 167–188.

Fisher, D., Hill, D., Grube, J., & Gruber, E. (2007). Gay, lesbian and bisexual content on television: A quantitative analysis across two seasons. *Journal of Homosexuality, 52*(3-4), 167–188.

Fiske, (1982). *Introduction to Communication Studies*. London: Routledge.

Fortune, A., & Reid, W. (1999). *Research in social work*. New York: Columbia University Press.

Gee, J. (2005). *An introduction to discourse analysis: Theory and method*. New York: Routledge.

George, A. (1959a). *Trends in propaganda analysis: A study of inferences made from Nazi propaganda in World War II* (a RAND Corporation Research Study). Evanston, IL: Row, Peterson and Company.

George, A. (1959b). Quantitative and qualitative approaches to content analysis. In I. De Sola Pool, (Ed.), *Trends in content analysis* (pp. 7–32). Urbana: University of Illinois Press.

Ginger, C. (2006). Interpretive content analysis. In D. Yanow & P. Schwartz-Shea, (Eds.), *Interpretation and method: Empirical research methods and the interpretive turn* (pp. 341–349). New York: M.E. Sharpe.

Glaser, B. (1978). *Theoretical sensitivity: Advances in the methodology of grounded theory*. Mill Valley, CA: Sociology Press.

Glaser, B., & Strauss, A. (1967). *The discovery of grounded theory*. Chicago: Aldine.

Gottschalk, L. (1995). *Content analysis of verbal behavior: New findings and clinical applications*. Hillside, NJ: Lawrence Erlbaum Associates.

Gottschalk, L., & Gleser, G. (1960). An analysis of the verbal content of suicide notes. *British Journal of Medical Psychology, 33*, 195–204.

Gottschalk, L., & Gleser, G. (1969). *The measurement of psychological states through the content analysis of verbal behavior*. Berkeley: University of California Press.

Gottschalk, L., & Hoigard, J. (1986). A depression scale applicable to verbal samples. *Psychiatry Research, 17*, 213–227.

Guba, E., & Lincoln, Y. (1989). *Fourth generation evaluation*. Newbury Park, CA: Sage.

Habermas, J. (1968). *Knowledge and human interest*. New York: Beacon Press.

Halvey, M., & Keane, M. (2007, May 8-12). An assessment of tag presentation techniques. Poster presented at the World Wide Web Conference, Banff, Alberta, Canada May 8-12, 2007. Retrieved from www2007.org/htmlposters/poster988/

Haney, W., Russell, M., Gulek, C., & Fierros, E. (1998). Drawing on education: Using student reflection surveys and drawings to promote middle school improvement. *Schools in the Middle, 7*(3), 38–43.

Harris, Z. (1952). Discourse analysis. *Language, 28*(1), 1–30.

Harris, Z. (1985). On grammars of science. In A. Makkia & A. Melby (Eds.), *Linguistics and philosophy: Essays in honor of Rulon S. Wells* (pp. 139–148). Philadelphia: John Benjamins.

Healey, L. (2001). *International social work: Professional action in an interdependent world.* New York: Oxford University Press.

Hill. C. (Ed.). (2011). *Consensual qualitative research: A practical resource for investigating social science phenomena.* Washington, DC: American Psychological Association.

Hochstetler, A., Murphy, D., & Simons, R. (2004). Damaged goods: Exploring predictors of distress in prison inmates. *Crime & Delinquency, 50,* 436–457.

Holcomb, L., Neimeyer, R., & Moore, M. (1993). Personal meanings of death: A content analysis of free-response narratives. *Death Studies, 17,* 299–318.

Holsti, O. (1968). Content analysis. In G. Lindzey & E. Aronson (Eds.), *The handbook of social psychology* (2nd ed., Vol. II, pp. 596–692). Reading, MA: Addison-Wesley.

Holsti, O. (1969). *Content analysis for the social sciences and humanities.* Reading, MA: Addison-Wesley.

Horton, E., & Hawkins, M. (2010). A content analysis of intervention research in social work doctoral dissertations. *Journal of Evidence-Based Social Work, 7*(5), 377–386.

House, E. (1991). Realism in research. *Educational Researcher, 20*(6), 2–9, 25.

Human Rights Watch [HRW]. (2012). *Old behind bars: The aging prison population in the United States.* Retrieved from www.hrw.org/reports/2012/01/27/old-behind-bars

Ife, J. (2001a). *Human rights and social work: Towards rights-based practice.* New York: Cambridge University Press.

Ife, J. (2001b). Local and global practice: Relocating social work as a human rights profession in the new global order. *European Journal of Social Work, 4*(1), 5–15.

Inaugural words. (2011, July 3). Inaugural words: 1798 to the present. *New York Times*. Retrieved from www.nytimes.com/interactive/2009/01/17/washington/20090117_ADDRESSES.html?_r=0

Johnston-Goodstar, K., Richards-Schuster, K., & Sethi, J. (2014). Exploring critical youth media practice: Connections and contributions for social work. *Social Work, 59*(4), p. 339–346.

Kais, D. (2011). *The quranic arabic corpus*. Retrieved from http://corpus.quran.com/

Kempe, C.H., Silverman, F.N., Steele, B.F., Droegemueller, W., & Silver, H.K. (1962). The battered-child syndrome. *Journal of the American Medical Association, 181*, 17–24.

Kimerling, R., Clum, G., & Wolfe, J. (2000). Relationships among stressor exposure, chronic posttraumatic stress disorder, and self-reported health in women. *Journal of Traumatic Stress, 13*, 115–129.

Kirk, J., & Miller, M. (1985). *Reliability and validity in qualitative research*. Newbury Park, CA: Sage.

Kohlbacher, F. (2005). The use of qualitative content analysis in case study research [89 paragraphs]. *Forum Qualitative Sozialforschung/Forum: Qualitative Social Research, 7*(1), Art. 21, http://nbn-resolving.de/urn:nbn:de:0114-fqs0601211.

Kracauer, S. (1952). The challenge of qualitative content analysis. *Public Opinion Quarterly, 16*(4), 631–642.

Kramer, B., Pacourek, L., & Hovland-Scafe, C. (2003). Analysis of end-of-life content in social work textbooks. *Journal of Social Work Education, 39*(2), 299–320.

Krippendorff, K. (1980). *Content analysis: An introduction to its methodology*. Newbury Park, CA: Sage.

Krippendorff, K. (2004). *Content analysis: An introduction to its methodology* (2nd ed.). Thousand Oaks, CA: Sage.

Krippendorff, K. (2013). *Content analysis: An introduction to its methodology* (3rd ed.). Thousand Oaks, CA: Sage.

Krippendorff, K., & Bock, M. (Eds.). (2008). *The content analysis reader*. Thousand Oaks, CA: Sage.

Krohne, H. (2002). *Stress and coping theories*. Retrieved from http://userpage.fu-berlin.de/~schuez/folien/Krohne_Stress.pdf

Kuckartz, U. (2012). *Qualitative Inhaltsanalyse: Methoden, Praxis, Computerunterstützung*. Weinheim, Germany: Beltz Juventa.

Kuji-Shikatani, K. (2004). *Using research for advocacy*. Retrieved from http://ceris.metropolis.net/pac/pac11.pdf

Kunkel, D., Cope, K., Farinola, W., Beily, E., Rollin, E., & Donnerstien, E. (1999). *Sex on TV 3: A biennial report to the Kaiser Family Foundation*. Menlo Park, CA: Kaiser Family Foundation.

Lalayants, M., Tripodi, T., & Jung, S. (2009). Trends in domestic and international social work research: A 10-year review of American research journals. *Journal of Social Service Research*, *35*(3), 209–215.

Landis, J., & Koch, G. (1977). The measurement of observer agreement for categorical data. *Biometrics*, *33*, 159–174.

Lazarus, R.S. (1966). *Psychological stress and the coping process*. New York: McGraw Hill.

Lazarus, R.S. (1991). *Emotion and adaption*. New York: Oxford University Press.

LeBreton, J., & Senter, J.L. (2008). Answers to 20 questions about interrater reliability and interrater agreement. *Organizational Research Methods*, *11*(4), 815–852.

LeCompte, M. & Preissle, J. (1993). *Ethnography and qualitative design in educational research* (2nd ed.). San Diego, CA: Academic Press.

Lee, M.Y., & Zaharlick, A. (2013). *Culturally competent research: Using ethnography as a meta-framework*. Pocket Guides to Social Work Research Methods Series. New York: Oxford University Press.

Lombard, M., Snyder-Duch, J., & Bracken, C. (2002). Content analysis in mass communication: Assessment and reporting of intercoder reliability. *Human Communications Research*, *28*(4), 587–604.

Mann, C. (2003). Observational research methods. Research design II: cohort, cross-sectional and case control studies. *Emergency Medicine Journal*, *20*, 54–60. Retrieved from http://emj.bmj.com/content/20/1/54.full.pdf

Marting, M. S., & Hammer, A. L. (2004). *Coping Resources Inventory Manual-revised*. Menlo, CA: Mind Garden, Inc.

Maschi, T. (2010a). *Culturally Responsive Sociodemographic Questionnaire–Prison* (CRSQ-P). New York: Be the Evidence International.

Maschi, T. (2010b). *Prison Stress and Coping Scale-Short* (PSCS-S). New York: Be the Evidence International.

Maschi, T., Baer, J., & Turner, S. (2011). The psychological goods on clinical social work: A content analysis of the clinical social work and social justice literature. *Journal of social work practice*, *25*(2), 233–253.

Maschi, T., Marmo, S., & Han, J. (2014). Palliative and end-of-life care in prisons: A content analysis of the literature. *International Journal of Prisoner Health*, *10*(3), 172–197.

Maschi, T., Sutfin, S., & O'Connor, B. (2012). Aging, mental health, and the criminal justice system. *Journal of Forensic Social Work*, *2*(2/3), 162–185.

Maschi, T., Viola, D., & Koskinen, L. (2015). Trauma, stress, and coping among older adults in prison: Towards a human rights and intergenerational family justice action agenda. *Traumatology: An International Journal* (special issue on Trauma, Aging, and Well-Being). Published online March 2, 2015.

Maschi, T., Viola, D., & Morgen, K. (2014). Unraveling trauma and stress, coping resources, and mental well-being among older adults in prison: Empirical evidence linking theory and practice. *Gerontologist, 54*(5), 857–867.

Maschi, T., Viola, D., Morgen, K., & Koskinen, L. (2015). Trauma, stress, grief, loss, and separation among older adults in prison: the protective role of coping resources on physical and mental well-being. *Journal of Crime and Justice, 38*(1), 113–136. doi:10.1080/0735648X.2013.808853

Maschi, T., Viola, D., & Sun, F. (2013). The high cost of the international aging prisoner crisis: Well-being as the common denominator for action. *Gerontologist, 53*(4), 543–554. doi:10.1093/geront/gns125

Maschi, T., & Youdin, R. (2011). *Social worker as researcher: Integrating research with advocacy*. Boston: Pearson.

Maxwell, J. (1996). *Qualitative research design: An interactive approach.* Thousand Oaks, CA: Sage.

Mayer, S. (2009). Using evidence in advocacy. In A. Thomas & G. Mohan (Eds.), *Research skills for policy and development: How to find out fast* (pp. 264–274). Thousand Oaks, CA: Sage Publications.

Mayring, P. (2000). Qualitative content analysis [28 paragraphs]. *Forum Qualitative Sozialforschung/Forum: Qualitative Social Research, 1*(2), Art. 20, http://nbn-resolving.de/urn:nbn:de:0114-fqs0002204

Mayring, P. (2007). Designs in qualitative orientierter Forschung. *Journal für Psychologie, 15*, 2. Retrieved from www.twoja-zaloga.pl/index.php/jfp/article/view/127/111

Mayring, P. (2010). *Qualitative Inhaltsanalyse, Grundlagen und Techniken* (11th ed.). Weinheim: Beltz, UTB.

McHugo, G., Caspi, Y., Kammerer, N., Mazelis, R., Jackson, E., Russell, L., . . . Kimerling, R. (2005). The assessment of trauma history in women with co-occurring substance abuse and mental disorders and a history of interpersonal violence. *Journal of Behavioral Health Services & Research, 32*(2), 113–127.

Mickelson, J. (1995). Advocacy. In R.L. Edwards & J.G. Hopps (Eds.), *Encyclopedia of social work* (19th ed., pp. 95–99). Washington, DC: National Association of Social Workers.

Mieses, J. (1929). Kassovsky's concordance to the Mishnah. *Jewish Quarterly Review, New Series, 20*(2), 143–150.

Miles, M., & Huberman, A. (1984). *Qualitative data analysis: A sourcebook of new methods.* Beverly Hills, CA: Sage.

Miles, M., & Huberman, A. (1994). *Qualitative data analysis: A sourcebook of new methods* (2nd ed.). Thousand Oaks, CA: Sage.

Miles, M., Huberman, A.M., & Saldaña, J. (2014). *Qualitative data analysis: A methods sourcebook* (3rd ed.). Thousand Oaks, CA: Sage.

Mislevy, R. (2004). Can there be reliability without reliability? *Journal of Educational and Behavioral Statistics, 29,* 241–244.

Morgan, D.L. (1993). Qualitative content analysis: A guide to paths not taken. *Qualitative Health Research, 3,* 112–121.

Morse, J. (1994). Designing funded qualitative research. In N. Denzin & Y. Lincoln (Eds.), *Handbook of qualitative research* (pp. 220–235). Thousand Oaks, CA: Sage Publications.

National Association of Social Workers (NASW). (2008). *Code of Ethics.* Washington, DC: Author.

Neimeyer R. (2001). *Meaning reconstruction and the experience of loss.* Washington, DC: American Psychological Association.

Neimeyer, R., Fontana, D., & Gold, K. (1983). A manual for content analysis of death constructs. *Death Education, 7,* 299–320.

Neimeyer, R., & Sands, D. (2011). Meaning reconstruction in bereavement: From principles to practice. In R. Neimeyer, H. Winokuer, D. Harris, & G. Thornton (Eds.), *Grief and bereavement in contemporary society: Bridging research and practice* (pp. 9–22). New York: Routledge.

Neuendorf, K. (2002.) *The content analysis guidebook.* Thousand Oaks, CA: Sage.

Neuendorf, K. (2007). *Computer content analysis programs.* Retrieved from http://academic.csuohio.edu/kneuendorf/content/cpuca/ccap.htm

NVivo 9.0. (2010). NVivo qualitative data analysis software; QSR International Pty Ltd. Version 9, 2010.

Osgood, C. (1959). The representational model and relevant research methods. In I. de Sola Pool (Ed.), *Trends in content analysis* (pp. 33–88). Urbana: University of Illinois Press.

Oxman, T., Rosenberg, S., Schnurr, P., & Tucker, G. (1988). Diagnostic classification through content analysis of patent's speech. *American Journal of Psychiatry, 145,* 464–468.

Padgett, D. (1998). *Qualitative research methods in social work.* Thousand Oaks, CA: Sage.

Patton, M. (1980). *Qualitative evaluation methods.* Newbury Park, CA: Sage.

Patton, M. (1990). *Qualitative evaluation and research methods* (2nd ed.). Newbury Park, CA: Sage.

Patton, M.Q. (2002). *Qualitative research and evaluation methods* (3rd ed.). Thousand Oaks, CA: Sage Publications, Inc.

Pearlin, L., Schieman, S., Fazio, E., & Meersman, S. (2005). Stress, health, and the life course: Some conceptual perspectives. *Journal of Health and Social Behavior, 46,* 205–219.

Polkinghorne, D. (1988). *Narrative knowing and the human sciences.* Albany, NY: State University of New York Press.

Popping, R. (2010). Some views on agreement to be used in content analysis studies. *Quality and Quantity, 44*, 1067–1078.

Pyett, P. M. (2003). Validation of qualitative research in the "real world." *Qualitative Health Research, 13*, 1170–1179.

Randolph, K., & Myers, L. (2013). *Basic statistics in multivariate analysis.* Pocket Guides to Social Work Research Methods Series. New York: Oxford University Press.

Reagan, J. (2010). Attribution and interpretive content analyses of college students' anecdotal online faculty ratings: Students' perceptions of effective teaching characteristics. Dissertation Abstracts International Section A: Humanities and Social Sciences, 71(6-A), pp. 1907. AAINR60735

Reeser, L.C. (2009). Educating for social change in the human service profession. In E. Aldarando (Ed.), *Advancing social justice through clinical practice* (pp. 459–476). Mahwah, NJ: Lawrence Erlbaum Associates.

Reichert, E. (2003). *Social work and human rights: A foundation for policy and practice.* New York: Columbia University Press.

Reichertz, J. (2010). Abduction: The logic of discovery of grounded theory. Forum: Qualitative Social Research, 11(1), unpaginated online document. Retrieved from www.qualitative-research.net/index.php/fqs/article/view/1412

Reisch, M. (2009). Legislative advocacy to empower oppressed and vulnerable groups. In A.R. Roberts & G.L. Greene (Eds.), *Social workers desk reference* (2nd ed., pp. 545–550). New York: Oxford University Press.

Riffe, D., Lacy, S., & Fico, F. (2005). *Analyzing media messages: Using quantitative content analysis in research.* Mahwah, NJ: Lawrence Erlbaum.

Ritsert, J. (1972). Inhaltsanalyse und Ideologiekritik. Ein Versuch über kritische Sozialforschung. Frankfurt: Athenäum Fischer Taschenbuch Verlag.

Robinson, W. (1951). The logical structure of analytic induction. *American Sociological Review, 16*(6), 812–818.

Rorty, R.M. (1979). *Philosophy and the mirror of nature.* Princeton, NJ: Princeton University Press.

Rosenbaum, P. (2010). *Design of observational studies.* New York: Springer.

Rourke, L., Anderson, T., Garrison, D., & Archer, W. (2000). Assessing social presence in asynchronous, text-based computer conferencing. *Journal of Distance Education, 14*(3), 51–70.

Royce, D. (2013). *Research methods in social work* (5th ed.). Belmont, CA: Thompson/Brooks Cole.

Rubin, A., & Babbie, E. (2010). *Research methods for social work* (7th ed.) Belmont, CA: Brooks-Cole.

Saldaña, J. (2009). *The coding manual for qualitative researchers.* Thousand Oaks, CA: Sage.

Sandelowski, M. (2000). Whatever happened to qualitative description? *Research in Nursing and Health*, *23*, 334–340.

Sandeloskwi, M., & Barroso, J. (2003). Classifying the findings of qualitative studeis. *Qualitative Health Research*, *13*, 905–923.

Schreier, M. (2012). *Qualitative content analysis in practice*. Thousand Oaks, CA: Sage.

Schreier, M. (2014a). Qualitative content analysis. In U. Flick (Ed.), *The Sage handbook of qualitative data analysis* (pp. 170–183). Thousand Oaks, CA: Sage.

Schreier, M. (2014b). Varianten qualitativer Inhaltsanalyse: Ein Wegweiser im Dickicht der Begrifflichkeiten [59 Absätze]. *Forum Qualitative Sozialforschung/Forum: Qualitative Social Research*, *15*(1), Art. 18. Retrieved from http://www.qualitative-research.net/index.php/fqs/article/view/2043

Shrout, P., & Fleiss, J. (1979). Intraclass correlations: Uses in assessing rater reliability. *Psychological Bulletin*, *86*, 420–428.

Singer, J. (2006). *Stirring up justice: Writing and reading to change the world*. Portsmouth, NH: Heinenman Publishing.

Sowers, K., & Rowe, W. (2007). *Social work practice and social justice: From local to global perspectives*. Pacific Grove, CA: Brooks/Cole.

Stevens, S. (1946). On the theory of scales of measurement. *Science*, *103*(2684), 677–680.

Stolarova, M., Wolf, C., Rinker, T., & Brielmann, A. (2014). How to assess and compare inter-rater reliability, agreement and correlation of ratings: an exemplary analysis of mother-father and parent-teacher expressive vocabulary rating pairs. *Frontiers in Psychology*, *5*, article 509. Retrieved from www.ncbi.nlm.nih.gov/pmc/articles/PMC4063345/pdf/fpsyg-05-00509.pdf

Strauss, A., & Corbin, A. (1998). *Basics of qualitative research: Techniques and procedures for developing grounded theory* (2nd ed.). Thousand Oaks, CA: Sage Publications.

Strong's exhaustive concordance. (2013). Retrieved from www.biblestudytools.com/concordances/strongs-exhaustive-concordance/

Tesch, R. (1990). *Qualitative research: Analysis types and software*. Abingdon, UK: Routledge-Falmer.

Thomas, A., & Mohan, G. (2007). *Research skills for policy and development: How to find out fast*. Thousand Oaks, CA: Sage Publications.

Thompson C., McCaughan D., Cullum N., Sheldon T.A., & Raynor P. (2003). Increasing the visibility of coding decisions in team-based qualitative research in nursing. *International Journal of Nursing Studies*, *41*, 15–20.

Tripodi, T., & Potocky-Tripodi, M. (2007). *International social work research: Issues and prospects.* New York: Oxford University Press.

Tutty, L.M., Rothery, M., & Grinnell, R. (1996). *Qualitative research for social workers.* Needham Heights, MA: Allyn and Bacon.

United Nations. (1994). *Human rights and social work: A manual for schools of social work and the social work profession.* Geneva: United Nations Centre for Human Rights.

United Nations. (2012). Report of the United Nations High Commissioner for Human Right. Substantive session, 23-27 July, 2012, Geneva.

Van Maanen, J. (1983). *Tales from the field: On writing ethnography.* Chicago: University of Chicago Press.

Vicini, S. (1993). Subjektive Beratungstheorien. Bernische Erziehungsberaterinnen reflektieren ihre Praxis. Bern: Lang.

Viera, A., & Garrett, J. (2005). Understanding interobserver agreement: The kappa statistic. *Family Medicine, 37*(5), 360–363.

von Glaserfeld, E. (1984). An introduction to radical constructivism. In P. Watzlawick (Ed.), *The invented reality: How do we know what we believe we know?* (pp. 17–40). New York: W.W. Norton.

Weber, R. (1984). Computer-aided content analysis: A short primer. *Qualitative Sociology, 7*(1/2), 126–147.

Weber, R. (1990). *Basic content analysis* (2nd ed.). Thousand Oaks, CA: Sage.

Wisse, J. (1989). *Ethos and pathos: From Aristotle to Cicero.* Amsterdam: Adolf M. Hakkert.

Willis, F., & Carlson, R. (1993). Single ads: Gender, social class, and time. *Sex Roles, A Journal of Research, 29*(5/6), 387–404.

Wolfe, J., & Kimerling, R. (1997). Gender issues in the assessment of posttraumatic stress disorder. In J. P. Wilson & T. M. Keane (Eds.), *Assessing psychological trauma and PTSD* (pp. 192–238). New York: Guildford.

Wolfe, J., Kimerling, R., Brown, P. J., Chrestman, K. R., & Levin, K. (1996). The Life Stressor Checklist–Revised. In B. Stamm (Ed.), *Instrumentation in stress, trauma, and adaptation* (pp. 198–200). Northbrook, IL: Sidran Press.

World Health Organization [WHO]. (2012). *Ageing and life course.* Retrieved from www.who.int/ageing/projects/elder_abuse/en/

Wyatt, D. (2012, June). *Gay/lesbian/bisexual television characters.* Retrieved from http://home.cc.umanitoba.ca/~wyatt/tv-characters.html

Yang, S.C., & Chen, S-F. (2006). Content analysis of free-response narratives to personal meanings of death among Chinese children and adolescents. *Death Studies, 30*, 217–241.

Zhang, Y., & Wildemuth, B. (2009). Qualitative analysis of content. In B. Wildemuth (Ed.), *Applications of social research methods to questions in information and library science* (pp. 308–319). Westport, CT: Libraries Unlimited. Retrieved from https://www.ischool.utexas.edu/~yanz/Content_analysis.pdf

Zimbalist, S.E. (1977). *Historic themes and landmarks in social welfare research.* New York: Harper & Row Publishers.

Znaniecki, F. (1934). *The method of sociology.* New York: Farrar & Rinehart.

Index